The NUMERHYTHMS PSYCHOLOGY BY NUMBERS *Series*

NUMERHYTHMS

The Code of Life

Psychology by Numbers

By Susan Schöning

The Soul Lighthouse Publishers

Published by: The Soul Lighthouse in Munich, Germany
Copyright: Susan Schöning, 2013
First published: First Edition 2013
Cover art: Under license from iStockphoto

All rights reserved. No part of this publication may be reproduced, stored in a retrieval system, or transmitted, in an form or by any means, without the prior permission in writing of The Soul Lighthouse, or as expressly permitted by law, or under terms agreed with the appropriate reprographics rights organisation. Enquiries concerning reproduction outside the scope of the above should be sent to the Rights Department, The Soul Lighthouse, at the address given on www.thesoullighthouse.com.

You must not circulate this book in any other binding or cover and you must impose this same condition on any acquirer.

ISBN: 978-3-9816440-0-5

This book is dedicated to all my clients, past and present.

You have all been, and continue to be, the most precious teachers and guides. Many of you have become friends and soul companions.

Thank you for allowing me to be part of your life's journey.
With endless gratitude, I thank you for being part of mine.

Foreword 1
   A Spiritual Journey 2
   Downloading from the Universe 5
   Meaning of Life 8
Section One - Introduction to Numerhythms 10
   Numbers are already part of your everyday life 10
   What if numbers were movie actors? 15
   The numbers: Revealing different facets of who we are 16
   Which set of numbers do we work with? 18
   What's in a name? 18
   Understanding the Basic Codex 21
   Where it all begins: The Date of Birth 22
Section Two - The Meaning of The Numbers 27
   ONE: Sacred Masculine 27
   TWO: Divine Feminine 30
   THREE: The Eternal Child 33
   FOUR: The Principle of Balance 36
   FIVE: The Adventurer 39
   SIX: The Nurturer 42
   SEVEN: The Purpose of Life 45
   EIGHT: Control and Achievement 48
   NINE: Old Soul 51
   Master Numbers: 53
   ELEVEN: New Consciousness 54
   TWENTY-TWO: The Master Builder 57
   THIRTY-THREE: The Master Teacher 59
Section Three - Calculating Your Personal Numerhythms 63
   What your date of birth reveals about you 63
   So what information does it carry? 64
   Life Path 67
   Skills & Talents, Karmic Lessons 72
      ONE: Initiator, Leader, Director 74
      TWO: Mediator, Counselor, Social Worker 75
      THREE: Visionary, Creator, Inventor, Designer, Sales Person 77

    FOUR: Builder, Balancer, Organizer, Routine and Order ____ 78
    FIVE: Motivator, Persuader, Change Agent, Communicator ____ 80
    SIX: Nurturer, Home Builder, Healer, Best Friend _____ 82
    SEVEN: Analytical, Specialist, Seeker of Truth, Detective _____ 84
    EIGHT: Control, Delegator, Manager, Professional, Judge _____ 85
    NINE: Humanitarian, Teacher, Soul Artist, Multi-talented _____ 88
    ELEVEN: Artist, Psychologist, Actor, Radical, Celebrity _____ 90
    TWENTY-TWO: Architect, Master Builder, Visionary, _____ 91
    THIRTY-THREE _____ 94
Triggers, Sabotage and Shadows Values. Dreams of deepest desire. _ 94
    ONE: Trigger and Sabotage Value _____ 96
    TWO: Trigger and Sabotage Value _____ 98
    THREE: Trigger and Sabotage Value _____ 100
    FOUR: Trigger and Sabotage Value _____ 103
    FIVE: Trigger and Sabotage Value _____ 105
    SIX: Trigger and Sabotage Value _____ 107
    SEVEN: Trigger and Sabotage Value _____ 109
    EIGHT: Trigger and Sabotage Value _____ 111
    NINE: Trigger and Sabotage Value _____ 113
    ELEVEN: Trigger and Sabotage Value _____ 115
Paradigm _____ 116
What exactly is a paradigm? _____ 118
    PARADIGM ONE _____ 120
    PARADIGM TWO _____ 120
    PARADIGM THREE _____ 121
    PARADIGM FOUR _____ 121
    PARADIGM FIVE _____ 122
    PARADIGM SIX _____ 123
    PARADIGM SEVEN _____ 123
    PARADIGM EIGHT _____ 124
    PARADIGM NINE _____ 124
    PARADIGM ELEVEN _____ 125
    PARADIGM TWENTY-TWO _____ 126
    PARADIGM THIRTY-THREE _____ 127

- Section Four - Your Soul Purpose ... 128
  - Life Purpose or Dharma Number ... 128
  - SOUL PURPOSE: ONE ... 131
  - SOUL PURPOSE : TWO ... 133
  - SOUL PURPOSE : THREE ... 134
  - SOUL PURPOSE : FOUR ... 136
  - SOUL PURPOSE : FIVE ... 137
  - SOUL PURPOSE : SIX ... 138
  - SOUL PURPOSE : SEVEN ... 140
  - SOUL PURPOSE: EIGHT ... 141
  - SOUL PURPOSE: NINE ... 143
  - Master Numbers ... 144
  - SOUL PURPOSE: ELEVEN ... 145
  - SOUL PURPOSE: TWENTY TWO ... 146
  - SOUL PURPOSE: THIRTY THREE ... 148
- Section Five - Working with Universal Energy ... 151
  - Predicting Future Events ... 152
  - The Universal Year ... 153
    - ONE Universal Year ... 157
    - TWO Universal Year ... 157
    - THREE Universal Year ... 157
    - FOUR Universal Year ... 157
    - FIVE Universal Year ... 158
    - SIX Universal Year ... 158
    - SEVEN Universal Year ... 158
    - EIGHT Universal Year ... 159
    - NINE Universal Year ... 159
  - Personal Year Cycles ... 160
    - ONE Personal Year ... 161
    - TWO Personal Year ... 162
    - THREE Personal Year ... 163
    - FOUR Personal Year ... 164
    - FIVE Personal Year ... 165
    - SIX Personal Year ... 166

    SEVEN Personal Year 167
    EIGHT Personal Year 168
    NINE Personal Year 169
    Remember 170
  Personal Month and Day 171
  Personal Day 173
    ONE Days 173
    TWO Days 174
    THREE Days 175
    FOUR Days 176
    FIVE Days 177
    SIX Days 179
    SEVEN Days 179
    EIGHT Days 180
    NINE Days 181
    ELEVEN Days 182

Section Six - Putting it all Together 184
  Case Study 184
  Step One: The Life Path 184
  Step Two: Fleshing the LIFE PATH out 187
  Step Three: The Soul Purpose 191
  Step Four: Working out the Universal and Personal Year Cycle 194

In Conclusion 199
  But wait… There's more!!! 199
  A sneak preview into Advanced Secrets of Intuitive Numerology .. 201
    About Compound Numbers 201
    Working With Time and Place 202
    Past Life Secrets 202
    Reading a Time Line 202
    Missing Numbers 203
  A New Journey 203
  Acknowledgments and Thanks 204
  About the Author 206

Foreword

If you had told me when I was in school that one day I would end up working with numbers, I would have laughed at you in complete disbelief.

I was the kid who hated maths. While everyone else in the class seemed to have at least some understanding of the subject (well enough, at least, to pass) I might have been learning Double Dutch! Those equations in Algebra had me stumped. Geometry made only slightly better sense, and as for book-keeping and accounting – well, perhaps the less said the better!

To this day, I still add and subtract by counting on my fingers, and when one of the kids brings maths problems home I am very adept at passing the buck to my husband. We have an agreement in our house; I get to help with all the interesting homework like language, art, biology and history. He gets all the science stuff like chemistry, physics… and maths!

Once I left school, my working environment took me far from away the linear, logical world of numbers. First as a nurse, later as a medical journalist and public relations consultant, and now as an Intuitive Counsellor and Energy Healer, I have found that other skills are far more fulfilling (and natural to me) than bringing endless streams of data to order.

One of my good friends is a book-keeper. She says she loves the symmetry and flow, the balance and order of working with numbers. The satisfaction she feels when her balance sheets add up is enormous; it makes her feel that she has found the perfect place for everything. When things don't add up, she feels irritable, stressed and tense and is unable to relax until she has found the problem and fixed it.

The beauty, she says, of working with numbers is that if you know where to look you can always fix everything and anything. Life becomes tidy and predictable and it works.

I have tried to understand how she feels… perhaps it's a bit like finding the exact fit of words to create the perfect phrase for an article that I am writing, or having a particular insight into a client's problem that unlocks an issue they have been grappling with forever.

The world makes sense to different people in different ways, I told her, and feeling relieved that I have such capable mathematical geniuses around me to help me through the daily challenges that figures and facts bring into the equation, I happily got on with living my non-structured, counting on my fingers (while biting on my tongue), kind of life.

So how did this mathophobe get to spend most of her working day surrounded by numbers? How did someone who couldn't put two and two together in a coherent fashion end up so intrigued by numbers that she sees them dancing throughout every aspect of her life?

A Spiritual Journey

It was a spiritual experience some 20 years ago that would change my life – and the way I would work with my clients - forever.

I have always been intuitive and held a deep awareness of energy and past and future events. One of my earliest memories is of speaking with my brother Michael shortly after he had been killed in a car accident. He and my elder sister had gone to stay with my grandmother who lived in another town; because I was so young at the time (I was only 6) I had stayed behind.

Michael came and sat on the edge of my bed, and told me that he was going to be going away and explained to me what had happened. I remember running to my mother and telling her that Michael had been killed by a car, and her telling me not to be silly; he was perfectly fine, he was only going to be away for a few days. It was just a horrid dream, that was all, she said as she put me back to bed.

The telegram came the next morning and confirmed that it hadn't been a bad dream after all. In every respect it was a very real living nightmare.

From that moment on I seemed to be able to sense things that were going to happen beforehand. A baby (and whether it would be a boy or a girl) before the mother knew she was expecting. A death. An accident. I would be able to walk into a room and feel the energy of the room, and know if there had been an argument, or if someone was lying or hiding a deep depression or sadness.

And not only could I sense the energies, there were times when I could see movement, see colors pulsing and swirling around people. I was born with a lazy eye, which means that my eyes sometimes look in different directions and at different focal points, which as you can appreciate means that I have an altered perspective and a unique depth (or lack of depth) of vision. I hated it as I was growing up as it made me the object of much teasing and taunting from other kids on the playground. Much later, however, I learned that it was actually *because* of this eye problem that I was able to see the energies and colors so easily.

I grew to be quite a serious child, spending a lot of time on my own immersed in my own world. I remember talking to friends as a young girl of about 8 or 9 about some of the things that were 'normal' in my world, only to have them laugh and mock, and so I learnt very quickly not to talk too much about it. It might have been my normal but it certainly wasn't normal for most of the kids I was growing up with.

As I grew into my teens I had an urging, a desire to find God. I knew that there was more, oh so much more than the physical world around us, and I began a conscious searching to discover how I could connect with it and really be able to know and understand it.

I began my journey by exploring Christianity but soon learned that this ability that I had, this "awareness" was considered to be evil, negative, dark. If I was filled with God I was told, my disturbing abilities to see and feel things would disappear. The more I was filled with the Holy Spirit, the less I would be afflicted by these 'dark gifts'.

But the more I prayed, the closer I felt to God, the more my abilities seem to expand not lessen. I struggled for years with the concept that I was evil because of this extra-sensory awareness that I had, that I was somehow marked by the devil, and I prayed harder and harder to lead a God filled life. Of course, I now know that the more we immerse ourselves in the energy of the Divine, the more the Divine works and moves through us. It made sense that my abilities would expand as my energy filled with God. How could it be otherwise?

I moved on from Christianity, discovering and exploring Alternative Religions, becoming fascinated and intrigued by how many ways we humans have developed to connect with the Source of Life, with Spirit. I was drawn to the lives and teachings of those masters and saints who had reached enlightenment, irrespective of which religion they followed, and knew that they had achieved something that I craved for my own life. Enlightenment. Awareness. Knowledge of the Divine. More and more I felt drawn to Mysticism and Metaphysics. Perhaps the answers I sought lay here?

It was at this stage in my late twenties that I met an Indian Guru and Mystical Master in Johannesburg, South Africa. I had been going through some very rough patches in my marriage and business, and someone had suggested this Master would be able to help.

I clearly remember sitting opposite a slight man dressed in yellow robes. While he was doing his reading I was mesmerized by the swirling colors of Violet, Magenta and Gold pulsating around his head and shoulders in time to his breath and body movements. For the first time I felt comfortable enough with someone to ask what these colors were that I saw on people, and animals, and trees. I asked him why his colors were so much more beautiful and glorious (the most beautiful I had ever seen) than those of other people who often seemed to have dark or heavy colors around them.

This man looked deep into my eyes - at the time I felt that he was boring into my very soul, and examining who I was at the deepest level of my existence. Then he asked me if I wanted to train with him. He explained that what I was seeing was the Aura, and if I could see it in my normal everyday life then I needed to be trained.

(Up until that stage, I just called it The Colors; I had no idea what an Aura even was!)

I turned up for my first training evening full of nerves and trepidation. By the end of the evening, I was hooked. I knew that this man was connected to the Divine; I wanted what he had.

I spent many years studying with him, absorbing and learning everything he had to say. He showed me that my ability was a Gift, not a Curse, and one that I could develop, train and expand with consciousness, humility and meditation.

He taught that all the energy of everything we know and *also that which we do not yet know*, exists at some level within the Universe in what he called 'pools of consciousness'. If we can raise our vibration to resonate at the same level of that consciousness, we can reach a level where we are able to access any knowledge or information or even awareness of past, present and future events. It was not a question of being psychic, he maintained. It was a matter of raising our vibration to resonate at the same vibration as that pool of consciousness. All information of every possible subject, from healing, to psychic events, to medical knowledge, to metaphysics - you name it, it exists out there in a pool of energy. All we had to do, he said, was discover the trigger that would raise our vibration to the level where we could automatically access the information with these pools of consciousness and bring it through into our daily lives.

DOWNLOADING FROM THE UNIVERSE

A great deal of time was spent in meditation, learning different techniques to raise our energy field in order to connect with the Divine. The journey was always towards God and enlightenment – any expansion of spiritual gifts was simply a bonus along the way. The goal was God, not psychic ability. I had found the teacher I was looking for.

I had recently been initiated in Kriya-Yoga, a specific meditation technique, when *it* happened.

I had been lying on the bed one evening, in that blissful half dozing state between resting and sleeping when I found myself being dragged at tremendous speed through a screaming wind. What was happening to me? I was being separated from my body and the sounds were terrifying. Nothing I had ever experienced before had ever been anything like this.

Suddenly I became aware that my brother Michael was there with my father and grandmother. Relax they said, let it happen, it's safe. And in truth, there was no fighting it. It swept me away and I was powerless to resist.

The screaming wind turned into a tornado of words, letters and numbers, swirling around faster and faster until they surrounded me in a blurring vortex of energy. I could hardly breathe with the sounds and sights that were bombarding my senses, steadily increasing in tempo and pitch and hammering into my third eye. It started to throb, the pressure increasing until it really began to hurt, the pain rapidly becoming excruciatingly painful. It felt as though a funnel was being forced into my brain through my third eye, and this chaos of numbers and letters pouring directly into my head. The right side of my brain felt as though it were expanding to three, four, five times its normal size as it absorbed the pulsating stream of data. I felt fat, engorged, swollen with it all.

And then, just as suddenly as it had started, it stopped. I descended into welcome darkness, and fell into a deep sleep.

The next morning I woke to a blinding headache, and a deep sensitivity to light and sound. It took a while before I could eat and drink normally; my stomach was upset, food tasted funny. I knew that something had happened the night before, but had no idea what 'it' was all, what it all meant – if anything.

It was only a few days later that 'it' suddenly manifested. A client arrived for an appointment (I worked as a psychic intuitive and energy healer) and I found myself asking for her date of birth, something I had never done before. As she gave me her dates, the numbers started to dance across the page, patterns forming on the paper in front of my eyes. By looking at the numbers and the patterns they were forming in front of me, I suddenly felt myself plunge headlong into a 'pool of consciousness' as my Master had so often referred to the Morphic Field. I knew things about her life, past and present that I normally would not have picked up. I could see immediately where her challenges were, what her life purpose was, what her biggest stumbling blocks were.

It was as though I were standing on the top of a tall building, looking down at her life, and from this vantage point of heightened perspective, I could see her relationships and likely future choices and events. The more the numbers danced on the page, the more energy I could see moving and the more information I was able to tap into about this lady who was sitting in front of me.

As I read her, I could feel the energy within me expanding as knowledge poured through me – I was vibrating, throbbing, pulsating with the power of this energy and I couldn't get the words out quickly enough. They were tumbling over each other in their haste to pour out of my mouth and into her ears.

And then just as powerfully as it had begun, the feeling of expansion and extra awareness passed. I continued with the reading and healing in the same manner I would have done in the past, only now with a much deeper insight into whom she was and what she needed than I had ever experienced with a client before.

As she left, I realized that I had no recollection of what I had told her. The information was not mine, it was hers, and having tapped into that pool of knowledge to give her the information that she needed to hear at that time, it left me to rest.

Until the next client. And the one after that. And the one after that.

Suddenly my readings took on a completely new dimension and energy as I connected with the numbers. They danced and twirled and sang across the page, speaking to me in a new love language that I had never heard before, giving me access not just to a pool but to an entire *ocean* of consciousness that left me longing to swim in it all day long.

From that day on, my practice exploded. Soon, my diary was full, and then I had a waiting list for months in advance. Obviously something powerful was at work here.

That 'power' crept into every area of my life. Soon I was seeing patterns and synergies at work everywhere: In the parking lot, in queues at the tax office, in shopping centers. Surface meanings and limited perspectives gave way to deeper and more profound insights, as each number and number sequence held its own energy, its own frequency, and its own vibration. Each number combination delivered a unique message, and tasted exquisitely different. Some patterns sparkled with vibrantly colorful signatures of enormous dynamism and charisma, while others moved with heavy, dense movements that were lethargic, sluggish and energy sapping.

I was hooked. Completely, totally, absolutely hooked. This was beyond intriguing. This was hypnotic, mesmerizing, captivating… and I wanted more.

MEANING OF LIFE

I discovered what so many people had tried to explain over the years, that numbers had a beauty, a simplicity and clarity to them – but wow, I'm not sure they meant in this sense?! Here was a language that I had somehow never heard before; there was such elegance and truth here, such beauty and power. From that time onward it became a central focus of my life. It changed the way I interacted with clients and did readings, certainly. But this new language taught me how to live my own life, with new meaning and awareness. I have spent the last 20 odd years, using and delighting in this Gift that was downloaded from the Universe. It has given me enormous joy and meaning. I have listened as the song of numbers have brought clarity and insight into my own life, and have watched with amazement and humility as it brings a sense and form to the lives of my clients. And I am even more in awe of the power of The Divine, and of the knowledge that exists out there in the Universe, just waiting for us to tap into if only we know how to. (Oh and in case you were wondering: No, I didn't become a mathematical genius overnight – I still count up on my fingers!)

SECTION ONE

Introduction to Numerhythms

I suppose at this point it would be expected that I explain the tradition and history of numerology and to encourage you to see this as a science and art that has intrigued and captivated mystical and intellectual minds for centuries.

But my introduction to numerology was anything but logical and traditional; rather it was explosive, colorful, absorbing, demanding my entire attention and energy, and so I decided that I would far rather take you on an intuitive discovery of the numbers at this point.

If you could feel the magic and mystery unfold the way I did, I *guarantee* it will change the way you see and relate to numbers forever. If I can capture just a little tiny bit of the excitement and energy of the music that each number makes, perhaps you would also long to join in the dance with me.

Numbers are already part of your everyday life

Truly they are. They crop up in our everyday language; we use them not just to convey a mathematical value or amount - as in: 'how much for these three lemons? Oh, that will be $1.29 please', or 'would you like one or two fried eggs for breakfast this morning?' (or even for the technically minded amongst us, 'the square root of PI is 1.772453851…') - but we also use them to convey meaning and color, mood and emotion.

We are all tuned into the subconscious language of numbers from the minute we learn to talk. Our language is peppered with numbers and we all instinctively understand the underlying characteristic or energy they imply.

If I ask you to think of a pair, you automatically know I am talking of two, together, relationship, partnership. The very word evokes visions of friendship, support, team worker, someone who is able to get on with people, comfortable, domestic. Most of us have an old comfortable pair of jeans that fit just so, or an old sweater that we feel ourselves relaxing into the minute we slip our (two) arms into the sleeves. As I am writing this I am wearing a dog eared pair of slippers which are beyond threadbare and worn out, but I cannot bring myself to throw them away. Why? Because I have worn them in, and they fit my (two) feet perfectly. Two conjures feelings of comfort and support and fitting together, and we all understand that this is so. It is the space a relationship moves into when the fiery passion dies down, and true love starts to grow instead. Comfortable, sustaining and supportive.

An individual on the other hand is always one, solitary, able to stand alone and move forward independently, capable of unique thought and the ability to 'make his own mind up'; a trail blazer, out on his own, creating his own path. It's the man in charge, the 'buck stops here' divisional manager, the one who decides how the rules of the game work and who ensures that everyone plays according to the rules that he has made. A bit like Clint Eastwood in all those old cowboy and cop movies that he did back in the (my) day – strong, silent but oh boy did he mean business and get things done! His modern day counterpart would probably be someone like Daniel Craig in his version of the James Bond role.

Already you can see that one is the epitome of the male energy, the man of the house, the boss, the leader, the one who says how things are going to get done, and then gets out there and does it. Likewise we can see that the two is his female counterpart, supportive, nurturing, building relationships, domestic. On a subconscious level, these are the qualities and characteristics we all understand when we start thinking of these numbers having personal qualities and attributes.

When one and two get together as they so often do, they join their energy to create the child of numerology – the three. Because three is a 'bit of one and a bit of two' it is sometimes unpredictable and uncertain. It needs the support and structure and gentleness of the two but, like the stubborn toddler, also wants to be independent and make his own decisions. We talk about 'two's company, three's a crowd' to describe the unsettling, vivacious, unpredictable energy the three can bring to a steady and stable twosome. Like the child it is, the three demands attention. 'Look at me, notice me, see me, experience me!' is the refrain of the three energy. Is it any wonder that when we think of three, we sometimes think of 'too much to handle' !

Four is the number of balance and stability, and we all immediately think of structure and reliability when we think of that number. Tables and chairs have four legs, and are stable and solid. They are able to support our weight, to be functional. Houses have four corners, which means we can rest a roof on the walls to cover us and provide security and shelter. It denotes a certain law and order, a predictability that is safe and appealing. There are four seasons to the year, and they provide an inexorable proof that the world continues as it has always done, in the order and rhythm that we understand. We instinctively know where we are with a four energy because of the very balance it evokes within us.

What about the five? Like the three, it's a non-conformist, not balanced, not predictable. Whereas with numbers like 2 or 4, 6 or 8, five just doesn't fit into any mould at all. No matter how much the five strains to conform itself into a box with four solid walls, it simply cannot do so. There is always some part of it rebelling against fitting into an imposed structure. Think about it for a moment: if you draw a box with four sides it occupies a neat contained space. Now draw another box with five sides. The only way you can make a five sided box fit into a four or six sided structure is to make it very small and contained. You need to restrict it from moving or growing in order to make sure it fits into the order and balance of a 'regular' box.

Now when I tell you that a five energy is the classic anti-establishment icon, the non-conformist, the quintessential James Dean in 'Rebel without a Cause' it makes absolute sense. In order to conform with 'normal' it needs to keep small and stay restricted, which as well we know is manageable for a while. Fives have the difficult task of trying to fit into a world where they don't always fit, to function within the 'accepted' structure, and to keep themselves walking a straight and narrow path in an effort to stop themselves from rebelling against it all completely!

People the world over have an instinctive perception that seven is the number of Other Worldly matters, of the Mysterious, of the Unseen World. We talk about the number seven as being part of that 'mysterious veil' that separates our world from the next, matters to do with the spirit and the soul, not matters pertaining to flesh and blood, or of being grounded in the here and now. Many of us were taught as kids that 'God made the world in six days (the number of diligent, consistent effort and hard work!) and on the seventh day he rested'.

In fact we even talk about being 'at sixes and sevens' when we are confused about something. Is it because intuitively we are aware that they are opposing energies - that the one is all about the physical realm of what can be seen and touched and felt, while the other tries to describe a realm that we have no way of quantifying or understanding from an earthly perspective?

If I asked you to come up with a character that resembled your personification of the number seven, who would it be? Merlin from the tales about King Arthur and the Knights of the Round Table? A modern-day Dumbledore straight out of Harry Potter? A version of Alistair Crowley? Or an Intuitive Empath who can hear the voices of Angels?

What about the number six? For me it would be the farmer who gets up with the sunrise and toils the land all day long, and who goes to bed with the sunset… only to get up tomorrow and the day after that, and the day after that, to do it all over again, come rain or shine, sleet or snow. It is the Quarter-Master in the Army, the man who ensures that all the tools, provisions, supplies and requirements for the army are available whenever they are needed. He works long and hard hours, generally unseen and unsung, far away from the battle lines. It was Napoleon who said that "a successful army marches on its stomach" and it is the job of the Quarter-

Master to keep that army fed so that it can be successful. A classic, responsible six energy.

It really is no wonder that we understand the phrase 'at sixes and sevens' to be one of confusion and uncertainty. The statement describes two completely different energies!

Eight is a number that belongs to the world, and has been linked to money and money fortune so often in Chinese Mythology, that we automatically think of it as a strong number that denotes power in finances. Everyone knows that if you get a lucky eight in your fortune cookie that it's a good omen for your bank balance!

Nine as a number denotes completion and folding back in on itself.

We count up to nine, and then our digits take us full circle back to one again, as we head into 10, 11, 12 and so on. Nine is the only number that no matter how many times you multiply it, the digits will always add up to nine.

9 x 1 = 9

9 x 2 = 18. 1 +8 = 9

9 x 3 = 27. 2 + 7 = 9

9 x 4 = 36. 3 + 6 = 9

And so on and so on.

It carries an energy of divine mystery. It takes nine months for a human pregnancy to complete, and then we give birth to a perfectly formed, wondrous new being, complete in its own wisdoms and mysteries. We talk about going 'the whole nine yards' when we do something properly the first time around, and everything has been taken into account; we are on 'cloud nine' when things go well, or to describe a state of blissful happiness.

The number nine is a sacred number in most spiritual and religious traditions, whether saying the Catholic rosary or chanting Vedic or Buddhist mantras – it represents the bridge between the real world, and the divine mysteries, a bridge that we all need to cross at some point in our lives to reach understanding and knowledge. It is the ultimate energy of transformation, the unknowing or reluctant hero who starts of an quest, or on a cause – we start off with one quality or understanding, but at the end of the journey find that we have been transformed or transmuted into something else entirely, and that our journey has changed the journeys of others around us.

WHAT IF NUMBERS WERE MOVIE ACTORS?

I have always thought that numbers have color, sound and yes, even typical character or personality traits.

ONE: Daniel Craig in James Bond, Clint Eastwood in Dirty Harry; Angelina Jolie in SALT.

TWO: Molly, Ron and Ginny's mother in the Harry Potter series; Robin Williams in Mrs.Doubtfire.

THREE: Peter Pan; Jodie Foster in Nell; Robin Williams in Patch Adams; Johnny Depp as Captain Jack Sparrow in Pirates of the Caribbean.

FOUR: Steve Martin in Father of the Bride.

FIVE: Bruce Willis in the Die Hard series; Tom Cruise in the Mission Impossible series.

SIX: The Farmer in Babe, Tom Hanks in Saving Private Ryan.

SEVEN: The little psychic boy in Sixth Sense; Keanu Reeves in Constantine; the Demon Busting Brothers in the Supernatural series on TV.

EIGHT: Michael Douglas in Wall Street; Meryl Streep in The Devil Wears Prada.

NINE: Neo in the Matrix Trilogy; John Carter in the Terminator movies; Harry Potter in the Harry Potter series; Katniss Everdeen in The Hunger Games.

As you read the above list of movie characters, maybe you can start to associate colors and sounds to the numbers. For instance, for me the number THREE will always have the soundtrack of The Pirates of the Caribbean sweeping me away irresponsibly to sail the seven seas with Johnny Depp. Who cares about the bills and routine of daily life when THAT song starts to dance in my head and I can go swash-buckling into the sunset?

Mention a FIVE to me and it's a toss-up between Mission Impossible and Bruce Willis fighting it out for my attention… and whoever wins, you just KNOW they are going to break all the rules! 'Come on, take a walk on the wild side!' says Bruce with that very cheeky grin of his, and I am very tempted to get into his getaway car and go racing off on a glorious adventure. SEVEN has that famous Twilight Zone music (do-doo-do-doo) complete with creaky doors and screeching owls going on in the background, while a TWO soundtrack for me sounds very much like Pachelbel's Canon in D, and makes me just want to reach out and caress my husband's hand, or squeeze my child's shoulder in love.

The numbers also carry an energy vibration and frequency that some see manifest as colors, patterns and shades. When you start to think of numbers as having personalities, energy and vibrations, they no longer are dry, flat facets on a page. They burst into life in an explosive riot of sound and texture, taste and feeling, movement and emotion.

In the next chapter as we go through the meaning of the numbers in intense detail, I would urge you to see if you can put a character or movie role to it, or associate a sound or color that makes the number *come alive* for you. It makes understanding the numbers so much more real when we dance *with* them and really *taste* and *experience* them, instead of just looking at them on a black and white page.

THE NUMBERS: REVEALING DIFFERENT FACETS OF WHO WE ARE

Before we get to grips with some of the calculations and the meanings behind the numbers, it is important to realize that there is so much more to us than just one or two facets of our personality.

We live many roles simultaneously in our lives and sometimes it's hard to know when one role stops and another one takes over, they overlap so much. At any moment in time, we inhabit at least four or more roles and each of these roles speaks with a different voice.

As I write this to you, I am a wife; a mother; a lover; a housewife; a therapist; a friend; a daughter; a sister; an author – and each of these roles exist comfortably within me, and in co-existence with each other, as I switch effortlessly between taking a call from client, (my work me), kissing my husband hello as he walks through the door at the end of the day, (my lover me) telling the kids that they've had enough TV and it is time for homework, (my parent me) and unloading the dishwasher as I start preparing supper, (my domestic goddess me).

It's the same with everyone. It is a fact of life.

We are comfortable with this concept of multi-tasking, and role playing because it describes what we all know to be true. We all have many functions, skills and talents that we call upon when we need them. Inside each of us is the career aspect, the love aspect, the hidden dreams and desires aspect, the soul purpose aspect.

My weak points, challenges, fears and insecurities are all hidden within me, as are my strong points, gifts, capabilities and power possibilities.

Inside of me I hold not just my talents and skills, but also those aspects of me that encourage or allow my talents and skills to be expressed. I am aware that there are parts of me that create obstacles which prevent me from getting out there and making things happen. Because of this, we cannot ever just look at one number in the numerological spread and say that it describes the whole person.

While one number may describe the general 'you' as you go through life, it is important to remember that it is only a general view, a broad outline. We only really start to colour in the picture and begin to see who *you really are*, when we look at you from *all* sides, and see who you are from a variety of different perspectives.

If we know how to look for it, we are able to see what your talents and skills are likely to be and how you will use them; we can see what type of challenges and obstacles you may face and whether you are likely to overcome them… or whether you will let them overcome you. One number may indicate your skills and talents, while another sequence will show how you respond in love. Still another number pattern will reveal all there is to know about your fears and insecurities, or secret dreams and desires.

Once you know how, you can examine a set of numbers and know whether someone is a realist, or a blue sky thinker; whether they are more likely to give into depression or anxiety; whether they are the proverbial "sell ice to eskimos type of salesman", a project manager, or a general all-rounder who manages the office like clockwork.

Now can you begin to imagine how useful this information could be in your daily life?

Which set of numbers do we work with?

Each numerologist will have their favorite method of working, one which allows them deeper insight and awareness.

Some prefer working with your name, while others prefer using the number patterns within your date of birth. Still others will use a combination of both alphabetical conversion and date of birth.

Because there is SO much information to present, we will only be discussing the Date of Birth in this book. At the end of this book you will find further details about the other books in this series of Intuitive Numerology.

What's in a name?

Our name is an energy that is given to us by our parents. We receive the name that we are going to carry throughout our lives as tiny babies; we certainly have no say in the matter and therefore no choice in the name we are destined to use to describe ourselves for our entire lives. Some of us are given five or six family names that resound with the echo of family history, belief and tradition, while others get given simply a first name and a surname.

Our name lays down a blueprint that describes the way the world sees us and expects us to behave… firstly our parents and close family; then as we grow older, our school and extended communities; and then as adults as we work our way through life. The world responds to us based in part to the vibration of our name and what it announces about us.

Over time, this expectation of behavior and subconscious realization of how the world shapes itself around our energy field becomes intrinsic to our developing personality, and we *become* what our name has *programmed* us to become. The name we are given symbolizes all that we grow into: it creates a shape for us to step into and grow up in.

I have always thought our name is a bit like a jelly mould. When you pour the jelly into the mould it is liquid and moveable, and it flows into all the crevasses and shapes in the container - in fact, you have to be careful when you pick it up that the hot jelly doesn't slosh all over the sides. At this stage you can dictate exactly what shape it is going to set into depending which mould you have poured it into – a fish or a shark, a flower or a tree, or just a simple jelly in a simple glass dish.

In time, as the jelly cools, it starts to set into the shape of the mould it was poured into. Anything that you have put into the jelly (fruit or biscuits) while it is still hot and liquid, slowly gets set firmly in place, unable to move as the jelly congeals into a yummy tasting gelatinous mass.

It's really the same with us. When we are born, we are pliable, impressionable, fluid, liquid… mouldable in other words. As with the biscuits or fruit that we throw into a jelly to change the taste, so experiences, events and happenings are also thrown into our mix where they slowly become firmly set in place, taking the form of thoughts, beliefs, habits, programming, traditions.

When you turn a jelly out of its mould, it still retains its shape - quivering deliciously – on the plate. When you turn *us* out of our moulding, we still carry the imprint of our early years and the shaping of the programme we were moulded into, with all our experiences and world views firmly held in place.

So what happens when we get married and our name changes – well for us women at any rate? It's like adding ice-cream to the jelly; it adds a new dimension of taste but the basic flavor can still be detected. A second marriage? It's like pouring chocolate sprinkles on top of the ice-cream that covers the jelly.

Adoption is seen as a special case. Some children are adopted at birth, and in many cases the adoptive parents have already been decided, the names have already been chosen, and so that child is 'born' into his or her name just as much as any other child. (However the child still carries the imprint of his biological parents, and this also needs to be taken into account when doing a name-based numerology reading.)

I was adopted by my step father when I was 9 years old, which meant that I had held one identity for 9 years, and then another for the next 12 years until my name changed by marriage. This is also a common occurrence in these days of the family-go-round, and so in instances like this the numerologist would work with all the names of the child, factoring in how many years they held that specific name energy.

I was born with one name, so that is my jelly. My early childhood experiences become the biscuits and the fruit, which changed the taste of the jelly. I was adopted into a new name at 9, so that became my ice-cream. I got married at 21, and added chocolate sprinkles to the mix. And then, I got remarried at 42, which poured a divine fruit juice all over it. The way I figure it, I am a regular fruit trifle!

Our date of birth signifies our first independent act on this planet. As we are born and take that first breath of air into our lungs, we breathe into our being an energy that carries the knowledge, power and vibration of *exactly* that specific moment and day in time. That vibration and energy pours into our lungs, and explodes into our tiny little bodies as each cell, each organ, indeed every level of our physical, mental, emotional and spiritual bodies respond to the glorious message 'Awake! Live! Become! Breathe!'

An exquisite vibration that only belongs to that unique moment in time starts to vibrate, pulsate and throb within us and we suck it all in that first breath where it plants a seed of all that we are and all that we can become.

And then in an explosion of noise we exhale our first breath, breathing the essence of *who we are* back into the Universe.

It is a statement, an acknowledgement of existence. 'Here I am' says that breath. 'this is who I am, I am HERE.'

It is like an ocean wave that fills us up as the energy of the Universe flows into us, awakening our own unique resonance. From that point on, every breath we take in comes from the Universe as it interacts with our unique energy blue-print, and every breath we out sends our energy signature back into the Universe, like a constant flowing in and out of energy.

** Both the name and the date however have powerful information coded into them, and when we work on both systems at the same time, we reveal the truth of the person at every level of who they are. In this volume, we are going to be focusing specifically on the secrets carried in your date and time of birth. If by the end of this book you are well and truly hooked, then make sure you watch out for Volume 3, which focusses on the energy carried in your name.

UNDERSTANDING THE BASIC CODEX

We dive headlong into this pool of numbers by first using the basic code, which is contained in your date of birth. Think of this code as the first jump into the water; once you are wet all over then you can start to learn basic swimming techniques, adding more and more complicated strokes and breathing mechanisms until you emerge on the other side as an Olympic Champion Swimmer.

It's the same with Intuitive Numerology. We start with the basic code first to pull you in, adding more and more complex patterns and sequences until you emerge on the other end as an Adept!

We can read your personality, see what health problems you may encounter, what type of childhood you are likely to experienced and how you responded to challenges and obstacles in your life. We can see whether you will be an early whizz kid or a late bloomer, if you will be lucky or unlucky in love, and what your life meaning and soul purpose are.

We can read the events and experiences that make up the past, present and future of your life. In short, we can see who you are, at your deepest core – as long as we know where to look, and how to interpret the information that you find there.

Some people are skeptical that a series of numbers associated with the letters of your name or the date of your birth can give insight into your experiences, your challenges and dreams, or even foretell how you will live your life and what your future will be.

Yet the facts speak for themselves however, and even the skeptics become converted when they realize just how accurate the information is from a seemingly random sequence of numbers!

WHERE IT ALL BEGINS: THE DATE OF BIRTH

You will notice that I use the European standard in writing dates of birth. You can quite easily change this to the American standard style, as it makes no difference to the end calculations.

A friend of mine had her baby on the 2 February 2002. If we wanted to find out about the child's energy in more detail we would simply need to add all of those numbers together to reach a single digit. First of course we write it digitally, which would become 2.2.2002

Then we add all these digits together, as follows:

2 + 2 + 2 + 0 + 0 + 2 = 8

This is a simple enough number, as it adds up to a single digit.

We would then turn to descriptions and meanings of the number 8 (described in great detail under Section 2) and read through the levels of interpretation there to discover more about the child's various qualities.

Easy, isn't it?

However, what if we have a more complicated date of birth, namely anyone who was born in the last century?

Let's use the 3 September 1975 as an example to illustrate how you would work with a more complicated date of birth. We would write it first in its digital format, i.e.: 3.9.1975, which of course would then become:

3 + 9 + 1 + 9 + 7 + 5 = 34

In Numerhythms we use a further method of addition known as the "Fadic" system, or "natural addition" to reach the single digit that we need. This simply means we keep adding the numbers together until we arrive at one single digit.

Using the Fadic System, we continue to add the double digits of 34 together:

3 + 4 = 7

The single digit value for the date of birth 3 September 1975 is a 7. We can then turn to description of the 7, and read it to get our first glimpse of the person born on this day.

Remember at this early stage that this **BASIC CODEX** gives you merely a first glimpse, an overall image of the person. As we proceed through this book we will be learning that there are so many more facets to the personality than just a single perspective. We humans are complex creatures after all: No one digit could ever sum us up completely!

As you become more and more adept at the rhythms of the numbers, we discover that just as the final digit holds a meaning, so of course do the double digits. In our example not only does the 7 hold a meaning, but so of course do the 3, the 4, as well as the number 34. Double numbers are also called compound numbers, and we explore this concept in great detail in Book 4 of this series, *The Code within the Compound Numbers.*

In this book, as we start our journey through the numbers, we are only beginning to become aware of the wisdom behind the numbers, and so we will only be working with the single digit which is reached at the end of the Fadic Addition sequence.

But, as we delve deeper into the numbers and their patterns at a more advanced level, we start to realize that the *patterns of the numbers*, the *sequences that they are added up in*, and the *final resulting single digits* all hold meaning and mysteries for the initiated reader.

The trick in interpreting then is knowing what the numbers represent!

Are you ready to know more? Then get your notepad ready, grab your calculator (if like me you still count up on your fingers) and a couple of colored pens or pencils so that you can navigate between the different numbers easily.

To make this information easier to work with, I have divided it into sections for simple reference

Section 1: Your introduction to Numerhythms

Section 2: The Meaning of the Numbers, 1 – 9; The Meaning of the Master Numbers, 11, 22, 33

Section 3: Your Personal Numerhythms – understanding the truths and secrets revealed in your date of birth

Section 4: Your Soul Purpose

Section 5: Working with Universal Energy

Section 6: Putting It All Together

Section 7: In Conclusion

But before you read any further, calculate your LIFE PATH and reduce it to a single digit using the Fadic System.

Numerhythms The Code of Life

We calculate the LIFE PATH by adding:

For example, if you were born on the 3 September 1975, we calculate as follows:

$$3 + 9 + 1 + 9 + 7 + 5 = 34$$

However, we need to reduce the double number of 34 to a single digit, which we do by using Fadic Arithmetic, of adding them to each other:

$$3 + 4 = 7$$

The Life Code is 7.

Have you worked out your Basic Code? Right then… let's find out what it all means!

Quick navigation links

If your Life Code is a ONE, continue on page 27

If your Life Code is a TWO, continue on page 30

If your Life Code is a THREE, continue on page 33

If your Life Code is a FOUR, continue on page 36

If your Life Code is a FIVE, continue on page 39

If your Life Code is a SIX, continue on page 42

If your Life Code is a SEVEN, continue on page 45

If your Life Code is a **EIGHT**, continue on page 48

If your Life Code is a **NINE**, continue on page 51

If your Life Code is a **ELEVEN**, continue on page 54

If your Life Code is a **TWENTY-TWO**, continue on page 57

If your Life Code is a **THIRTY-THREE**, continue on page 59

SECTION TWO

The Meaning of The Numbers

ONE: Sacred Masculine

The number ONE symbolizes the principle of BEGINNING or INITIATION. It is ambitious, an achiever, and really comes into its own when it is allowed to be a leader and independent. Self-sufficient, inventive, stubborn, and dominant, this energy is masculine, focused, and rational.

Please note that when I say male energy it doesn't mean that you dash around acting Butch all the time! Male energy tends to be focused, strong, harder, decisive, forward thinking, whereas female energy is more often seen as softer, more nurturing, gentler, less urgent about pushing their decisions to the fore, more comfortable in the background than being on center stage under the spotlight. Of course, the spotlight is often where the ONE energy thrives.

ONEs can be quite fashionable, dressing smartly and appropriately for the situation, and they care about how they look. Not a slave of fashion by any means, but possessing rather a unique style and flair that sets them apart from the crowd, which in reality they are. Although they can be team players, ONEs prefer to work alone, and be responsible for their own productivity and achievements, not have their brilliance blanketed behind team efforts.

People with this energy often radiate with a dynamic energy, one that exudes strength, control, courage and creativity. If you are a ONE Energy, chances are that you can be a wee bit headstrong, are a natural leader and like to be in charge and call the shots. You don't like to be pushed around, and as you often have your own (generally) very good ideas about how things need to get done, people often leave you to get on with it and "do it yourself".

You are often seen to be a pioneer, and come across as intelligent and quick thinking. You seem to be capable bordering on efficient at whatever you undertake and certainly possess some strong qualities: individuality, originality, independence, courage, strength, creativity, authoritative, to name just a few! You often seek opportunities to display your strength and usefulness, wanting to create and originate.

You take pride in your abilities and achievements, and want to be recognized for them. Nothing wrong with that, but sometimes you are needy of constant recognition and have the danger of becoming overly boastful or egotistical about your abilities in order to get the level of validation and approval that you crave.

What it means though, is that you need to be assertive within and learn to value and acknowledge your own worth, as opposed to relying on others to validate you. Learning to stand alone and stand-up for what you believe in, are core lessons of the ONE energy.

Often you portray the image that you are very confident, very capable and sure of yourself… even at those times when you feel that you are quaking in your boots. Sometimes, if you are not careful, you can come across aggressive and arrogantly unreceptive to other people's thoughts and ideas, or the way that other people get things get done.

Intolerant and inflexible are words that may sometimes be used to describe you. In fact, at times you can be downright intimidating, and need to be aware that sometimes you can come over abrupt when you focus too much on the task at hand. This is a great quality if you are in a boardroom, finalizing a project or managing a group of staff members; it's not too great when you are in a love relationship and you end up "telling" or "controlling" and – let's be honest - "dictating" what you want your partner to do and exactly how you want it done. You have an ability to dominate situations and people; the home, the spouse, the family and the business, as you are far better in dealing with the facts at hand than the emotion of the situation. You must avoid being too critical and impatient of trifles, as this tends to irritate even the most easy going of partners.

If you commit to something or someone, you stand by them and follow it through, as long as it continues to make sense in the bigger picture to you. In a relationship you like to "wear the pants" and direct and manage the relationship and where it is going, but get turned off by too much emotion, clinging and dependence in your partner.

On the plus side, there is a great deal of honesty and loyalty in you; you are a loyal friend and an exceptionally loyal lover and partner. Fairness and honesty in a relationship is vital to you, and you expect your lover to treat you with the same openness and integrity as you do for him or her. You also have high standards in business, and cannot stand underhand dealings or non-disclosure, or feeling as though people are going behind your back. You trust people and expect them to be as straightforward and trustworthy as you are, and are truly shocked and disillusioned if they don't.

Because of their unique ability to focus in on the matter at hand, and almost to lose all track of space and time when absorbed with something that is important to them, the ONE energy holds the very real potential for mastery and excellence in whatever field they chose, if they apply themselves enough.

Other attributes of the ONE energy:

Out of balance, the ONE can become: A wee bit stubborn, headstrong, egotistical, blunt, ambitious, dominant, willful, impulsive, tyrannical, arrogant, bossy, intolerant.

In balance, the ONE is: Original, independent, unique, courageous, strong, creative, authorative, capable, self-sufficient, inventive, successful in the pursuit of excellence.

Personal Goals: Establishing individuality; being in control of the situation; making a name for themselves in their area of excellence, and being respected and acknowledged in their field.

Fears: Being overlooked; not using talents; becoming invisible or irrelevant or not respected; disappointment.

Success can come from: Writer, director, inventor, president, public figure, business owner, designer, creative, entrepreneurial and solitary pursuits.

TWO: Divine Feminine

The number TWO symbolizes the principle of coming together with another, of diplomacy, partnership, teamwork and support. TWOs are generally very aware of others' needs and strive to demonstrate friendliness, understanding and tact. Sometimes artistic, sometimes shy, TWOs also have the ability to be quite thorough in whatever project they undertake. This energy is feminine and magnetic.

When we say female, that is not meant to indicate that you have a propensity to waft around, limp-wristed, wearing kaftans and smoking cigarettes through pink cigarette holders! While male energy tends to be focused, strong, harder, decisive, forward thinking, female energy is far softer, more nurturing, and more gentle.

Often more concerned with how others are feeling than themselves, TWOs are naturally empathetic and supportive, genuinely interested in other people and what makes them tick. Understanding, loving, compassionate and tactful, people with a strong TWO energy will seek "win-win" situations where everyone can benefit.

The ability to see both sides of the story is a tremendous gift, and when the TWO energy is in balance, this is one of their greatest strengths. Diplomacy is a natural skill for most TWOs, as they are very patient and understanding. They make for wonderful listeners as they have an unique ability to focus in on others, which in turn makes them feel important and loved.

People sense your overwhelming desire for harmony. If you are a TWO then you know that you are sensitive and that arguments, tension and conflict will leave you drained. Because you hate conflict so much, you will go out of your way to avoid it, just to keep the peace - sometimes to the extreme of letting others have their own way even though it's really not what you want or is best for the situation. As a strategy in any situation, be it an intimate relationship or a working situation, it is effective in the short term. In the long term of course, all that happens is that you become the door mat for others' angers and frustrations which makes you want to avoid situations and people even more!

It's not to say that leadership isn't important, but making a contribution to the team effort is far more rewarding for you. Your motivation for life is centered on friendships, partnerships, and companionship. You want to work with others as a part of a co-operative team. You are persuasive, but in a very quiet way, never forceful

You present an image that you are a very pliable and easygoing person who would be very easy to get along with, appearing friendly and soft hearted. People are drawn to you because, among other reasons, you appear warm and unthreatening. Diplomatic, friend, artist, eternal peacemaker, gentle, insightful, sensitive, you have the ability to pour oil on rough waters and to soothe ruffled feathers. This part of your personality indicates that you can also be rather emotional. You are the type that makes really close friendships and keeps them forever, because you are so affectionate and loving.

Sometimes, though, your sensitivity can make you feel self-conscious, unappreciated, fearful and hesitant to take risks… and love most certainly is one of the biggest risks there is! The opposite sex is attracted to your gentle and attentive nature, yet senses the passion smoldering beneath your surface. You certainly have sex appeal, that's for sure, although you tend not be blatant and loud about it. People sense they will be cared for when they are in your arms.

You long for close and meaningful relationships, for harmony and cooperation with those around you and will go out of your way to try to create it with lovers, family and friends.

Because you come over gentle, softer, less threatening in the beginning, people may underestimate your strength, but this is a mistake. You can be nagging, manipulative and critical when you feel threatened, and in arguments when you feel vulnerable or exposed, can retreat behind sarcasm and manipulation in order to feel heard. Because of your sensitive nature there is the danger that you can sometimes over-react to a situation, or become over-sensitive, which means that you can get too hurt too easily. TWO energies that feel threatened have been known to attack with scathing comments and passive aggressive actions in a 'the best form of defense is attack' strategy.

Because you fear rejection, you may be timid or fearful, holding yourself back completely from living your life and making decisions, preferring instead to hide behind a carefully cultured image of Mr. Nice Guy, becoming way too easygoing and non-committal for your own good. Even worse, TWOs often hide their light in the shadows where it feels safer… but really isn't. All it creates is a profound sense of invisibility.

Learning to express your truth, and stand up for yourself is one of the key lessons that the TWO needs to learn. It is easier to walk away from a conflict, or an argument, or a stressful situation that's for sure, but it is not always the right thing to do. Sometimes in walking away from an argument, we leave a big piece of ourselves behind.

Other attributes of the TWO energy:

Out of balance, the TWO can become: Self-consciousness, fearful, hesitant, over-conscientiousness, bogged in the details, always putting others first to the point they get walked all over, manipulative, critical, nagging and sarcastic

In balance, the TWO is: peace-maker, diplomat, able to see all sides of the story, nurturing, compassionate, caring, loving, insightful, sensitive, intuitive, supportive, understanding, and charming.

Personal Goals: Feeling safe, establishing reciprocal relationships based on nurture, love and truth

Fears: Unknown, unplanned changes, being alone, making a mistake

Success can come from: Artist, technician, psychologist, spouse, healer, bookkeeper, nurse, teacher, parent, best friend.

THREE: THE ETERNAL CHILD

The number THREE symbolizes the energy of growth. When the initiating masculine power of the ONE unites with the germinating nurture, feminine energy of the TWO, the result is the fruitfulness and fertility, creativity and charisma of the number THREE.

It signifies union, a joining together in order to create something new and alive in its own right, with its own identity and its own direction, and so the THREE energy really symbolizes synthesis in action. It is the product of imagination and directed energy, of nurture and support, and the result is bold, colorful, vibrating, pulsating.

Sometimes youthful to the point of being childlike, this energy is captivating and attention grabbing as it strives to uplift and empower others. If there is one word that describes this energy when it is in its full power it would have to be this: enlivening.

Because the THREE is the product of ONE and TWO, it is often called the child in numerology. Think for a moment of a child's energy; they are vibrant, full of laughter and inquisitiveness, finding joy in the simplest of life's pleasures. An ice cream and a jump in the paddling pool are events to be enjoyed just as much as a birthday party or a trip to Disneyland. Children have short attention spans and flit from activity to activity, as their mood moves them – and anyone who has ever spent the day playing with a three year old will testify that they are bundles of constant, never-stopping energy.

This is a spontaneous energy which often is called childlike by others... full of life, spontaneous, uplifting, inspiring, and charming. Often extroverted and naturally optimistic, affectionate and giving, generous to the core. Anything goes, life is for the living, and others often find this social and easy-going outlook on life deeply attractive. THREEs love to play and have fun... vibrant, busy, active, FUN. When a THREE is in a good mood, their infectious laughter and smiles attract other people to them. Sometimes however, wit and humor can become flippant, blasé, even superficial. A THREE under pressure hates silences, and they have been known to just chatter on, simply to make some noise and fill up the space with some noise.

The child-like energy of the THREE expresses itself in wide eyed wonder, in the ability to feel and spread joy in the simplest of activities. THREEs can pour all their senses into the matter at hand, whether it be playing with sea-shells on the beach, or standing up giving a sales and marketing presentation, (or for that matter, having a drinking contest with the blokes at the Oktoberfest in downtown Munich). All well and good, but the flip side of this is that sometimes child-like wonder paves the downhill slide into childish irresponsibility and unaccountability, a character trait that can leave others gritting their teeth in frustration while they run around clearing up "your toys" afterwards.

If you are a THREE, you will need an outlet to express your creative, artistic or intellectual talents – and you certainly will be talented, with an urge to create. Some THREEs are brilliant cooks, others are fantastic dressmakers or able to landscape a garden or create beautiful homes. You are really good with words and certainly have the gift of the gab... whether playing, speaking, writing, singing or acting!

You can have the most brilliant of ideas, and get seized by projects and dreams, thinking and talking of nothing else for ages, but if you are not careful, that's all that will ever happen with them. THREEs are fantastic with coming up with new ideas, new ways of doing things, thinking laterally, seeing things outside the box. If you are honest with yourself though, you can talk way too much, and in fact talk yourself out of an idea before you even start it.

If you do get to start it, you do so with great motivation and intention. It's just, well, a little like a toddler not wanting to put their toys away at the end of the day, the THREE runs the risk of not finishing things. The energy and interest seems to fade away half way through, and before you know it, our THREE has been seized by the next brilliant idea and runs off full tilt at yet another tangent.

Because THREEs have an active mind and imagination, this seems to attract many opportunities throughout your life. When backed up by hard work and self-discipline, these qualities almost ensure your success; however… you run the risk of avoiding responsibility when you don't like the project or prospect in front of you. Enthusiasm leads to demotivation, apathy and laziness when you are no longer interested in something… or downright avoidance, when you are no longer interested in someone.

Because the THREE energy in numerology is shaped by the ONE (masculine) and the TWO (feminine), people play an extremely important role in your life. Some THREEs need to be living in a social whirl; others prefer the company of close friends as opposed to the big pulsating party on a Friday night. One thing is very clear however: what other people say and do has the power to affect how the THREE thinks of him or herself. You crave acceptance and inclusion. You want to be liked and loved by everyone, you want the invitation to join in the birthday party… and when you get it, feel good about yourself. What happens however when you feel excluded, or pushed aside, or you find that everyone else has been invited to the birthday party but your invitation seems to have gone missing in the post? It has the ability to make you feel less than, invisible, unseen and unwanted… and this shapes how you feel about yourself. This makes the THREE extremely sensitive, sometimes even vulnerable.

You don't respond well to criticism or "constructive advice", you have the tendency to lose self-esteem and feel insecure if people comment on your behavior or performance. Everyone has faults, and can do with advice and wisdom at times, but you do not like to hear that someone doesn't approve of you or what you do, and often will evade or avoid that person or situation rather than be near them again.

One of the biggest challenges for a THREE is to not allow the external world of people, things and events to shape, validate or substantiate you. Your worth does not depend on what others think of you; your worth depends on what you think of yourself.

Other attributes of the THREE energy:

Out of balance, the THREE can become: Prone to exaggeration, lack of direction, unfinished projects, sensitivity to criticism, laziness, apathetic, demotivated, inconsistent, insecure and immature, blaming others for the situations they find themselves in.

In balance, the THREE is: creative, social, easygoing, a visionary, funny and humorous, energetic, spontaneous, enthusiastic, powerful imagination, versatile, optimistic, playful.

Personal Goals: To create something that exists because of ME. To enjoy life, to stay as young as possible for as long as possible.

Fears: THREEs fear growing old and the loss of youth, restriction, boredom, being alone, making a mistake and being found out.

Success can come from: Motivator, coach, writer, musician, artist, parent, salesperson, marketing and advertising, chef, creative pursuits, communicator/all media.

FOUR: THE PRINCIPLE OF BALANCE

The number FOUR symbolizes the principle of putting ideas into form. It signifies work and productivity. The FOUR is constructive, realistic, traditional and cautious. It is the number of system, order, and management.

FOURs thrive on order and harmony, on stability and balance. This is the energy that reflects reliability, consistency, determination, and trustworthiness. Whereas some of the other numbers have the ability to get lost in "blue sky, out there thinking", FOURs are generally very realistic about life. If they are honest with themselves, they prefer the balance of conventionality and the rules governing tradition and order - because in predictability and convention lies the known element, which translates into safety, harmony and balance.

FOURs often feel that if they could just get all the apples on their apple cart to be balanced *just so*, then life would be just great. They get distressed if their metaphorical apple cart hits a bump in the road and all their apples spill to the ground, after they have so painstakingly put them in order

This is not to say that FOURs are boring and dull. Nothing could be further from the truth. A FOUR energy is more likely *to see life as it is*, not as others wish it could be, or used to be. Some people call that having no imagination; for the FOUR that means that they have their feet firmly planted in reality, with a strong view of what can be and what can't be achieved.

If you are a FOUR, then you probably have the ability to concentrate on the matter at hand. Others know that you can be utterly relied upon to be methodical, consistent, efficient and precise. "If a task is worth doing it's worth doing well first time" could be your motto… and that applies equally to all tasks, whether that be balancing the checkbook, managing the office, or cleaning out the cupboard under the sink.

A FOUR energy gets tremendous pleasure in reaching the end of a task and knowing that it is done and finished; half-finished projects and incomplete activities have the ability to drive you crazy. You would rather finish a project and know that it is done well, than leave it half way through.

Being a realist, you are concerned about security of the future, and it is important to you to either be a good provider and protector, or be in a relationship with someone who is. At heart, deep down, you have a belief that consistency and adherence to well-laid plans usually pays off in a comfortable and secure future. You are concerned about the security of your future and those you love.

Stability is vitally important – whether it be in a career, relationship, friendship or family context. You are just as unlikely to storm out of your job without having a back-up plan, as you would be to walk out on your partner if you had nowhere else to go.

You thrive on the intimacy, consistency, and the security a family provides.

At the heart of the FOUR energy is the craving to achieve balance and stability – and this can translate into walking deep ruts into some very well worn and familiar paths. FOURs like to sleep in their own beds at night, with their own pillow, in the known comfort of their own home; they can become creatures of routine to such an extent that they don't lift their heads to see if things could be done a different way.

Another FOUR saying could easily be: "if it's not broke, don't fix it… or in other words, why mess with a formulae that works?"

If you have a downside it is that you can be too rigid and narrow minded in your outlook, being too cautious to take risks, or deviate from a well walked path of safety and comfort. In love you prefer safety and security and reliability with a partner who keeps you in your comfort zone, rather than the heady excitement of new love. Because you often have a firm, even traditional idea of how relationships and family should work, any challenge to that self-imposed image can be threatening for you.

When challenged, you retreat back into the safety of routine, order, and balance and cautious… all energies that make you feel safe.

What is it that the FOUR needs to learn? That sometimes what appears to be safe and under control is simply a prison of your own making. FOURs need to step outside their box for a moment, and to consider whether they are allowing life to pass them by while they are keeping things "stable and balanced". The true power of the FOUR lies in being balanced in every respect: mind, body, emotion and spirit, and when that happens, the FOUR has the ability to reign supreme.

Other attributes of the FOUR energy:

Out of balance, the FOUR can become: Prone to rigidity, too cautious, limited viewpoint, unwilling to try new things, boring, stuck in a rut or routine, inflexible, unwilling or unable to see another's point of view.

In balance, the FOUR is: Able to focus and apply themselves to the matter in hand from beginning to end, determined, reliable, conscientious, practical, realistic, traditional, builder, doer, manager, capable, trustworthy, balanced.

Personal Goals: Safety, security, completion.

Fears: Sudden change, loss of stability, loss of control, being without resources.

Success can come from: Earth scientist, business owner, developer, lawyer, administrator, office worker, body worker, project management, parent.

FIVE: THE ADVENTURER

The number FIVE symbolizes the principle of energy, progression, and passion. It signifies the need for change, variety, and new growth. It thrives in the open and grows in the spotlight, but can wilt and crumble if kept in the dark for too long. The FIVE energy is the broadcaster, the communicator, the one who disseminates information, always asking questions. It is out-going, fast-moving, mercurial, active, dynamic and charismatic, capable of sweeping others along on a tidal wave of passion and change.

WOW! The epitome of progress and passion, thriving on change, variety and new growth. Unconventional and different, people can be persuaded and uplifted when a FIVE person speaks, or even when he just enters the room.

Often a very physical and sensual energy with loads of stamina to draw on, this person has the ability to "think on their feet". FIVEs are fast moving, creative, outgoing, freedom lover, adventurer, with an aura which literally screams out loud *"can do, let's go"*.

Daring, non-conventional, certainly unpredictable at times? Absolutely. Easily seduced by the world of the physical senses? Oh yes. Sometimes if we are being really, *really* honest, FIVEs are prone to over-indulgence. It may not be food or drink that gets this person's eyes shining either! At the one end of the spectrum, people with this energy are just as likely to be powerful sports people dedicating hours to endless honing and toning of the body beautiful, abstaining from alcohol, over the counter medications or any food with a higher than 3% fat content, as they watch their weight and external image with almost rigid fanaticism. FIVEs have been known to become fanatical about their house and person being decorated just so. (Ok, so they can be just a tad obsessive!). At the complete opposite end of the spectrum, FIVEs can be the proverbial couch potato or house slouch; the alcoholic who doesn't know when enough is enough, and who lacks the willpower to actually say "No!"; the drug addict who gives into addiction because it just feels "so good in that moment"; or even the Don Juan (or Femme Fetale) in their constant seeking of endless conquests to prove their insatiable virility to themselves and others.

Whether you are a gourmet cook, or muscle-pumped with a six pack, whether you have a beautifully designed home or are over fond of over-indulging your favorite senses, one thing is for certain: In both love and life, you can be passionate and generous, giving and sensual... yes, sometimes to the extreme. Jealousy and possessiveness are often part of your love language. You hate losing and sometimes feel insecure and unsure of yourself, unfavorably and unnecessarily comparing yourself to others. This can lead to mood swings... sometimes being so up that you can shape your future with power, and sometimes being so down and consequently feeling so insecure or worthless that you are overwhelmed by the pointlessness of it all.

If there is a lesson that the FIVE energy needs to learn is that they have the power and ability to be all they can be, to realize their own highest potential – but that they are their own worst enemy. They truly have the potential for self-destruction is as equal measure as they have the capacity for self-realization.

FIVEs would do well to remember this simple mantra: Whatever you put your focus on, grows; whatever you put your attention on, increases.

Because the FIVE is so strong, always moving and growing, the challenge is to make sure that it grows in the right way, constructively and positively, not negatively and destructively. This means that the FIVE has to be extra vigilant, extra conscious of the choices he or she makes, and *remember the reasons* why he made the choice in the first place.

The FIVE has huge amounts of willpower and stamina but, if you are really honest with yourself, you are also often prone to procrastination and self-delay when faced with a choice of pursuing something that feels good, versus doing some routine chore or activity. "Why waste a beautifully sunny day? I'll do that report tomorrow/ clean up tomorrow/ wash the car tomorrow!" FIVEs can be absolutely brilliant, this is true, but they can also be very undependable.

FIVEs need freedom and space, the promise of adventure, the lure of the unknown. Not for them a day of sitting behind a computer followed by the next 28 days in the month doing exactly the same thing – boredom sets in quite quickly, and as the soon as New and Exciting become Routine and Common-Place, the FIVE can become restless, sometimes even downright destructive in their need to get away from boring and into a space where they feel they can breathe!

One of your greatest gifts is your ability with language and words. You can hold an audience absolutely captivated when you open your mouth to speak, and, because you are not afraid of expressing yourself, this ability to talk and communicate can take you to very great heights in the public arena. You love the spotlight, even thrive on it. That's not to say you don't get nervous, but you know better than anyone that nervousness helps the adrenalin to kick in, and makes you give a better performance.

Make sure that you perform only when it's time to perform though. Because the FIVE is sometimes prone to exaggeration, passion, and charisma, there is the risk that life becomes one long performance. Prima Donnas should only step into that role when they are on stage, not play-act all the time. It wears everyone else out around them otherwise.

Remember, that you have a way of using words that can build and promote, uplift and persuade – or destroy and wound and maim. It is a powerful ability, and you need to be aware of the power of the spoken word with the ones that you love.

Other attributes of the FIVE energy:

Out of balance, the FIVE is prone to: Restlessness, procrastination or activity with no direction, lack of follow through, addictive or self-destructive/self-sabotaging behavior, drama queen, depression/what's the point, apathy, insecurity, self-doubt.

In balance, the FIVE is: Expansive, free thinking, influencer, adventurous, sensual, generous, dramatic flair, charismatic, dynamic, motivator, passionate, creative, good with words, Resourceful, magnetic, motivated, competitive.

Personal Goals: To win, to experience life to the maximum, to be seen and validated.

Fears: Growing old, not seeing the world, boredom, restriction, feeling suffocated, being unseen.

Success can come from: Public figure, developer, speculator, designer, journalism, news work, performer, change agent, trainer, public speaker.

SIX: THE NURTURER

The number SIX symbolizes the principle of nurturing, caring, and harmony in action. This energy needs stability with a solid home-base to feel truly comfortable. It is the teacher, trainer, parent, at its happiest when surrounded by familiar, friendly faces and conventional, well known surroundings.

The true SIX is rarely selfish, often thinking of others and how they are feeling, coping or managing with life. They go out of their way to help and support others, especially when they are in a relationship with them, to the point that they may take on the emotional or physical burdens of others unnecessarily, becoming worn out or overwhelmed in the process.

As long as they feel they are helping and appreciated, SIXs will bend over backwards to look after and support – but will retreat into resentment and silence if they feel that what they are doing is unappreciated, or worse, taken for granted.

If you are a SIX then you know that you operate best in known, predictable and safe situations, where you know the lay of the land and can anticipate how things will turn out. You are a whizz at organization and preparation, and love to be in charge but only from the "backroom". Whether you are organizing a dinner party or the army marching band, you like things to have a time, regulation and order to them. Things work better when they have been meticulously planned, and you don't like nasty surprises, which is why you try to be prepared for any eventuality.

You are a gracious host or hostess, going out of your way to look after every one and meeting their needs and desires. You also probably over-cater, way too much, to the extent that you are eating left-overs for days after the party!

Open and comforting when secure, nurturing and healing when balanced, you can become exceptionally opinionated and over-anxious when feeling threatened or insecure, sometimes to the point of being dogmatic and over-bearing, intolerant and completely inflexible. You have a very deep fear of being over controlled, of co-dependency, or being manipulated. In fact, if something worries you deeply, you dwell on it, and it can go round and round in your mind, driving you mad with anxiety and stress. When financial insecurity - or let's be honest, even when the mildest financial hiccup threatens - you can become rigid, overly disciplined and miserly to the point of becoming stingy and frugal.

At its worst extreme, SIXs never take a holiday; such a frivolous waste of money could be invested far more valuably in the pension plan or retirement scheme. Pushed to their limit, SIXs can become sticklers for routine and rules: Supper has to be served at 6pm, curtains get drawn at 7pm, and bed time is at 10pm. Routine brings a certain order and predictability to life, this is true - but be aware that it also can become very stifling and overwhelmingly severe and strict, crushing all the joy out of life, not only for you, but for those who share your life.

On the other, more positive end of the spectrum, when they have the space to grow and be, SIXs are caring and compassionate, with a great capacity to see fairness and compromise. If you are a six, then you are also utterly reliable, probably with a reputation for keeping your promises no matter what.

Friendship, love, and affection are high on your list of priorities for a happy life. Diplomatic, able to see both sides of the situation and retain perspective, you are very giving of love, affection, and emotional support.

In order to truly thrive, and not just simply survive in life, SIXs need a stable and solid home base, preferably one that is comfortable and gracious, beautiful and functional.

Sometimes however, because of their tendency to either "do too much" for the ones they love, or "to retreat into ruts of routine and regulation" they find it hard to achieve what they crave the most, which is a loving and giving partner, a happy and secure home life, a contented family. If you don't have it, finding it will become a huge focus in your life. If you are blessed enough to have it, then you will be romantic, faithful and very protective. You have all the characteristics that will make you a wonderful parent and a beautiful lover and spouse.

Possibly the biggest challenge facing the SIX energy is to not confuse being used and controlled by others with being loved or needed.

Other attributes of the SIX energy:

Out of balance, the SIX is: Rigid, inflexible, intolerant, resentful, withdrawn, stifling, strict, severe, and anxious.

In balance, the SIX is: Caring, just, fair, able to see both sides of the story, well organized, compassionate, reliable, domesticated, responsible, provider, service orientated, nurturing and loving.

Personal Goals: To provide for others' well-being, to create security and harmony, to love and be loved in equal measure.

Fears: Anxiety, being over controlled, codependency, guilt, not finding a partner, not being part of a family structure (however unconventional that family structure may be: sixes need to belong).

Success can come from: Parent, educator, caterer/ cook, nurse, body worker/health consultant, traditional professional, counselor, coach, manager, teacher, sergeant major.

SEVEN: THE PURPOSE OF LIFE

The number SEVEN symbolizes humanity's deep inner longing to find depth, meaning and spiritual connection. According to Maslow's Hierarchy of Needs, we humans are driven creatures: Firstly to find food, shelter, safety; secondly for a mate, family, sexual satisfaction. After we feel secure that these base needs have been met and have a reasonable degree of certainty that they will continue to be met, we are able to search for acceptance and belonging, for community involvement, for acknowledgement that who we are and what we do has value and worth in the eyes of those around us.

Once these creature-comforts for acceptance, material status and domestic achievements have been realized, we then turn to the deeper levels of life to understand who we are and why we are here. We seek to learn, to educate ourselves in things that really hold meaning or truth. It is at this level that we start to ask some very penetrating questions… "Who am I? Who am I going to spend my life being? What do I believe? What is my purpose? What am I on this planet to do?"

SEVENs want above all else to find their purpose for being on this planet. The SEVEN energy craves understanding and spiritual connection, however he or she defines those borders of spirituality to be. SEVENs search for the meaning of life, love and everything else. If you are a

SEVEN energy, you will know that as you pursue whether there is indeed a deeper meaning to life, you can sometimes appear different or even eccentric. You may even become a loner, craving solitude in which to find the inner voice. Your ability to analyze things in minute detail can lead to incredible insights and awareness, as you search for that which gives your life meaning, and direction, but be careful: You also have the tendency to over-analyze, picking over the bones with a fine-toothed comb which can keep you stuck in a situation, unable to move forward until you have analyzed things to the *nth* degree.

It is critical for you to discover what your purpose is in any given situation and, if you cannot grasp what it is you are meant to be doing with your life, you can become exceptionally frustrated with yourself and life in general.

If there is no purpose to an activity, then you will quickly lose the interest and desire to be involved, no matter how many promises of richness and fame have been dangled in front of your eyes. Likewise, even if there is no apparent material reward to something that you are doing, if it holds meaning and there is a worthwhile (in your eyes) reason to what you are doing, then you will pursue it with single-minded passion, moving heaven and earth to make it happen. Some people might look at you and scratch their heads in bewilderment, as they try to understand what really makes you tick.

People with a SEVEN energy, when they are focused enough, have an incredible ability to "reach the zone", that place within themselves where they are centered and super-concentrated, aware of what needs to be done and when it needs to be done by. This quality is what sets achievers apart from the rest of the crowd; it is a quality that signifies success and accomplishment, and we can see it manifest in sports people, in business achievers, in artists, in healers.

In fact, it could be said of a man with a SEVEN energy, that if he is absorbed in a specific task – whether that be up to his eyeballs on the computer with work, or watching Bayern Munich slaughter Man United on the football field – there is nothing his woman can do to distract his attention. Even Miss World, undulating seductively to the Dance of the

Seven Veils will not get him to look up until half-time, or he has balanced the spread sheet!

This desire for excellence is, well… excellent of course, but it can lead you to stop yourself before you get started; not letting the project go out until it is precisely just so (according to your exacting standards), or not letting the brochure go to the printers until it is absolutely picture-perfect in every last detail. Sometimes the SEVEN has to remind themselves to just let go, and let things happen, without trying to hyper-manage every last detail.

Because you have such very high expectations of what signifies success, you sting yourself and those around you with frustration, criticism and narrow mindedness when things don't pan out the way you had hoped. Admit it, you sometimes do have impossibly high standards, and can come over quite high handed and superior, intolerant and dismissive when these standards just aren't met.

It stands to reason that this energy can create its own stress, leading to anxiety at a mild level, billowing into full blown panic attacks when you feel that things are spiralling out of control.

Sometimes SEVENs can be overly attached to the past, becoming argumentative and rigid when disappointed or feeling vulnerable, or at the other extreme, becoming silent, withdrawn and over-anxious. SEVENs have been known to have explosions of temper, which are frightening to watch as they can become quite "incandescent" with anger.

Sometimes suspicious, holding their secrets deep within, finding it hard to trust others' motives, if our SEVENs really have a downside it is that they can be rigid, aloof, judgmental, and critical (even sometimes obsessive and addictive). On the plus side? SEVENs are perfectionist, thoughtful, spiritual and seeking to find an expression of life that they understand and resonate with.

In love you can be hard to please, so it is vital that your life partner reflects some of your desire to find purpose and meaning. Frivolousness is not for you; you would rather be alone than in a relationship that has no meaning.

Other attributes of the SEVEN energy:

Out of balance, the SEVEN energy is: Proud, narrow-minded, distant, rigid, overly connected to the past, argumentative, exploding into temper or lapsing into a deep silence, a perfectionist, a loner, withdrawing from soceity.

In balance, the SEVEN energy is: A seeker of truth, a specialist, inventor, thoughtful, spiritual, mentally capable of understanding and grasping deep truths, able to analyze with clarity, seeking perfection.

Personal Goals: To maintain control over life; to understand what their purpose is, Spiritual connection.

Fears: Failure to achieve standards, making a mistake.

Success can come from: Consultant, professor, analyst, sports specialist, individualist, observer, occultist, intuitive, mystic, investigation, detective, inventor, seeker of truth.

EIGHT: Control and Achievement

The number EIGHT symbolizes the principle of domination, control, and achievement. It is the executive decision-maker. The EIGHT is often more comfortable in the realm of material, tangible facts and so people often only see this side of their personality. The truth is though, that the EIGHT energy is truly exceptional as soon as it develops its spiritual connection and intuition, which it owns in bucket loads.

Strong, decisive, hard headed, materialistic, powerful – you can be all of these things. You are also hardworking, focused on the matter at hand, courageous, and analytical. Authority, confidence and the ability to motivate others to your way of thinking comes naturally to you.

You have the attitude that if you work hard you will get ahead in life; nothing in life comes for free; there is no such thing as a free lunch, and if something is worth doing it is worth doing well. All of this is true, and it makes you able to achieve any goal you set your mind to, (as long as you want it badly enough).

All of this can make you superb in the world where you wish to excel - be it as a strong contender in the business world, a leader in the career of your choice, as the director of some nursery school play, or even as the driver behind the church committee or tennis club. You have the ability to get the best out of people, to really pull their talents and skills out of hiding, which is a phenomenal skill in itself. This alone could become a powerful success strategy for you.

EIGHTs like to be autonomous, and to work under their own authority, whether that is at home or in the office. Their best work is achieved when they are left to set their own pace, and when they are able to work in silence and solitude. Sometimes this can be to your detriment – as you seek to work alone, you may find that you are missing out on vital people contact.

When it comes to love, EIGHTs sometimes need to learn that love cannot and should not be controlled, directed and packaged. Lovers do not want to be "problem solved", they do not want "solutions" presented to them. They want to discuss, to have conversations, to explore playfully, not be directed or managed. Lovers want to stand side by side, holding hands, being equal, not two steps behind; a lover wants to share in your life, not be delegated to!

As you enter into a love relationship or even a friendship relationship, it is vital that you remind yourself that it is ok to play, ok to explore, and certainly ok not to have all the answers all the time.

Because the truth is: Although you can inspire and lead, although you come across as generous, warm and exciting, you can also be intensely lonely, feeling as others don't understand you very much at all. You are sometimes too self-controlled, controlling how much of your emotions and feelings others get to see, and this can make you appear a wee bit rigid and just a tad stubborn.

EIGHTs need to learn how to play again, and how to lose themselves in the sensuality of life, how to have a good time simply for the pure pleasure of having a good time. Once you do this, and let go of the control you hold yourself under, you will add a depth to your make-up that completes you.

Once you are at home in the emotional and spiritual realm as well as the logical material realm, you will be truly remarkable, with so much to offer on every level.

Pushed to your extreme, you can become exceptionally stubborn, dominating, intractable, formal, stern and unmindful of authority and yes, sometimes judgmental and angry when things just spiral out of control. But in your full power, you are confident, strong, capable, and efficient and a natural leader with a good grasp of how to achieve anything you set your mind to.

Probably one of your biggest challenges is to learn compassion, tolerance, and justice… primarily for yourself, as you have the ability to judge yourself way too harshly.

Other attributes of the EIGHT energy:

Out of balance, the EIGHT becomes: Belligerent, manipulative, angry, judgmental, stubborn, dictatorial and overly materialistic.

In balance, the EIGHT is: Decisive, courageous, focused, and able to delegate and manage a project from the beginning through to its final completion. EIGHTs also exude professionalism, strength, are money orientated, able to solve problems and find solutions for anything. They are also great at organizing, have the capacity for success and achievement, and when in balance, are discerning and wise.

Personal Goals: To gain control over themselves and their environment, to achieve power and status.

Fears: Loss of prestige, being at the mercy of circumstances or of others less capable, being overlooked, not being recognized or considered worthy, losing control of the situation.

Success can come from: Any type of professional, business owner, publisher, contractor, engineer, financial analyst, judge.

NINE: OLD SOUL

The number NINE symbolizes the principle of a universal philosophy or consciousness. It is the dreamer, the accomplished individual who is able to feel at home on the stage acting and performing just as much as he can become absorbed by medicine, religion, societal politics… or in philosophy and metaphysics. It is the healer and educator, the one who always seems to have the bigger picture in mind, trying to achieve the 'greater good' for the benefit of others.

It is often called "the old soul" because this energy seems to have come into life with the ability to be aware, to be conscious, to tap into both past wisdom and future knowledge. Truly, when they stand in their full glory, these people hold the key to the treasure chest in their hands.

This energy is at its best when it is able to merge with the creative, intuitive and inspirational worlds. When he stands in a place where he feels not only comfortable but supported in his uniqueness, the NINE becomes compassionate, expansive and global minded, able to think and act for others. While the rest of us can worry too much about our own lives, and our own 'small' situations, the NINE is genuinely concerned for the collective state of mankind, conscious about the environment and the planet. Because of this, they often look for ways how to improve the experience and lives of others, giving advice and suggestions (often unsolicited) when they see a situation that can be improved upon.

The problem of course is that not everyone wants a solution, or advice given to them. We humans are funny that way, preferring often to bash our heads against a brick wall until we are black and blue all over before we learn our lesson. To have someone sitting on the sidelines and suggesting a different way of doing things, even though they may well be completely right, is not always conducive to changing behavior. When the advice is wanted, and the suggestions work out, the NINEs are the humanitarian hero of the moment; when it doesn't the NINE can be labeled as interfering, sanctimonious, condescending, smug and superior, labels that truly confuse them.

Susan Schöning

A dreamer, a humanitarian, a multi-talented personality that acts at its deepest level for the benefit of others… sounds too good to be true, doesn't it? And yet, and yet: NINEs often feel as though they are slightly out of step with the rest of the world. It's almost as if the world hears the beat of a different drum altogether, and marches in unison to the sound that *they* hear. NINEs will have to make the choice about whether to march in time with the rest of the world… or accept that their drum beats a different time and rhythm altogether, one that only they can hear.

Until they accept that they are unique, individual and sometimes apart from the rest of the crowd, NINEs can wear themselves out trying to fit in, trying to be the same as everyone else, all the while wondering what they are doing wrong and why they just can't seem to get this "going with the common flow" thing right.

As a NINE, once you realize that you are truly, truly exceptional, you are then able to step into that energy which allows you to change, not just you but everyone around you, for the good.

One of your biggest strengths is your desire to truly understand the point of view of others around you. You form opinions but these are generally open for discussion, and your "show me where I'm wrong" or "tell me your side of the story" can be very compelling and win you a lot of friends. However, when you feel that you have got the right answer, or get particularly stuck on a course of action (whether it is positive or negative) you can become very rigid in your belief and actions which makes you intolerant of other's input, coming over arrogant, aloof and superior to others' view points in the process.

In fact, if others disagree with you passionately, you have the tendency to become a martyr, feeling misunderstood or unwanted, unrecognized or non-effective, which drains you of energy and direction which in turn creates despair and uncertainty. This makes you withdraw and you have the ability to shut down for long periods of self-imposed isolation if you feel that "the world is against you". Behind the calm face you present to the world, you are deeply sensitive, vulnerable with a deep capacity for all aspects of emotion.

In love you can beautiful to be with on so many levels. You go out of your way to understand, to empathize, to love, to be compassionate, and you are loyal sometimes over and beyond the call of duty. But when you are disappointed or feel let down, or if your partner challenges your carefully nurtured beliefs and morals, you withdraw, becoming scathing or non-committal, disinterested and uninvolved.

You need to tell your partner not only what it is you want, but also what you expect and hope for in a relationship; just because you have a seemingly highly developed ability to intuit what others want, don't automatically expect them to become mind readers as well and simply KNOW what it is you want. You need to communicate your needs and desires.

Other attributes of the NINE energy:

Out of balance, the NINE becomes: Drifting, intolerant, able to lose focus, runs the risk of developing and keeping bad or self-destructive habits, condescending, smug, superior, sarcastic.

In balance, the NINE energy is: Understanding, communicating, influencing, sensitive to others around them and their needs. Nine energy is also seen as a generalist, multi-talented, teacher. It can be the humanitarian, the healer, artist, old-soul or actor.

Personal Goals: To make an impact in a big way; to protect the environment, the planet, the value of life.

Fears: Restriction of any kind, losing control of emotions.

Success can come from: Minister, occultist, health/body worker, counselor, artist/craftsperson, world/community leader.

Master Numbers:

In the last chapter I explained that we always reduce a double number using Fadic Arithmetic, until we reach a single digit. There are of course, exceptions to every rule and numerology is no different.

There are three numbers that we do not reduce ever, as they carry their own unique vibrational energy and resonance, and they are called Master Numbers.

These Master Numbers are: 11, 22, 33

Numbers that carry the same double number have a specific resonance as they heighten and exaggerate both the powers and challenges of the single number. Because they carry so much power, they can be hard to "wear" while the person is still growing up, and only really come into their full power and strength as the person grows older.

Some traditional numerologists will say that there are only 3 master numbers, namely – 11, 22 and 33 - and that when you reach numbers like 44 or 55 and so on, that you need to add them up using the Fadic system. I look at both patterns: the meaning of the double 4 or the double 5, and then the combined value… but that is an advanced method and is dealt with in great detail in *Advanced Secrets of Intuitive Numerology*.

ELEVEN: NEW CONSCIOUSNESS

The number ELEVEN symbolizes the principle of enlightenment. It colors everything with drama and has a visionary outlook, oodles of artistic sensitivity and a very sparkling energetic personality - most of the time. It is perhaps not always practical but, because it is able to see things from a unique perspective, it is often philosophical, certainly mystical, idealistic, expansive, big picture and hands on.

This energy has the potential to inhabit all of our human emotions, sometimes in rapid-cycling succession, moving from enthusiastic and energized, to compassionate and caring, to slow, depressed and apathetic. ELEVENs can also be very high-strung, intense, polarized (off and on), and completely unpredictable at times. Just when you think you've got an ELEVEN figured out, they change tangents and behavior at a speed that will leave you reeling!

Numerhythms The Code of Life

Wow! Life is certainly never dull with you around. You operate at full speed most of the time, whether you are up in the clouds or down in the dumps... and like your moods, you have the ability to fill your world and everything in it with either the vibrant, dramatic, joyful colors of your happiness, or the dark grey, blacks and browns of your depression and despair. One just has to look at your face, your shoulders or your body language to see what you are feeling deep inside. It's as impossible to keep that smile off your face when you are energized and creative, just as much as it is unlikely for you to smile when your world feels completely rainy and gloomy.

Intense, sometimes highly strung, sensitive to the extreme, you thrive off approval and recognition, and need to feel visible at all times in order to feel validated - otherwise you can crumble and disintegrate if you feel ignored. The danger is that you need outside approval to make you feel noticed and worthwhile, when you should have this knowledge and awareness inside of you. You are not as good as someone else makes you feel; you are good because you feel and know yourself to be. You are extremely sensitive, sometimes really hard on yourself, with the ability to judge yourself way harsher than anyone could ever dream of judging you.

You sometimes swing too radically between moods and emotions, between energy and lethargy, between the creation of good or destruction of everything that you have worked so hard to achieve. At its absolute extreme, people with ELEVEN energy can walk away from what promises to be a highly successful project in the proverbial 11th hour, just before it completes "because it just didn't have the right feeling for me anymore."

In business it can be hard for people to keep up with your fast changing pace and the speed with which you are able to think things through. Because of this, you may find that you are two steps ahead of everyone else... becoming frustrated by others who just don't seem to have the energy, inclination or wavelength if they slow you down. You crave movement, achievement, action. Not for you the 9 – 5 job with a punched in time clock, it would drive you nuts! You get bored easily, and love trying new and different just for the excitement of it all.

If you are working in a job where you can't see any progress, or any evidence that you are getting through to people, you can become really agitated, frustrated and disillusioned. What you do HAS to have meaning and value, not just for you but for the people around you, and if it does, you are energized and empowered by your work. If not? "Why bother?", you may shrug to yourself.

In love, you need your love partner to focus on you and to be available for you whenever you need him or her to feel important and loved. Passionate, moody, temperamental, extravagant, demanding, opinionated, charismatic, sparkling… all these words describe the different roles that you can play, at different times, in varying situations. But so too, do the words, compassionate, caring, sensitive, vulnerable, sensual, creative, and gentle with those you love and care about.

You love beauty, sensuality, creativity, and if you dig deep you will uncover the soul of the artist and the poet that lives with you. Dig even deeper and you have a spiritual being who craves connection with the Divine. Dig deeper still, and you uncover insight, intuition and a powerful psychic ability that leads to a desire to explore the occult.

You have the heart of the true idealist, and may believe there is more to life than we can ever know or prove… and secretly, if you are honest with yourself, see yourself showing people the way to that higher or deeper truth. This is something you have to believe in about yourself; you WERE born to reach out and show people how to connect, how to realize their full potential, how to be more than they ever believe they could be.

Other attributes of the ELEVEN energy:

Out of balance, the ELEVEN energy is prone to: Self-illusion or self-deception, isolation, allergies, over-stimulation, rapid cycling emotions, self-sabotage.

In balance, the ELEVEN energy is able to: Inspire, reveal higher truths, and transform people's inner lives. It is poetic interpretation at its best, seeing beauty everywhere, romantic. ELEVEN energy is also the artist, celebrity, highly energized, psychological, radical, sensitive, idealist.

Personal Goals: Living the dream, becoming that Somebody Special.

Fears: Drudgery, restriction, ugliness, boredom, repetition, suffocation.

Success can come from: Media star, poet, inventor, psychologist, minister, designer, society figure, beauty queen, occultist.

TWENTY-TWO: THE MASTER BUILDER

The number TWENTY-TWO symbolizes the principle of precision and balance. It is the energy of the MASTER BUILDER, the one who can conceive of and achieve that which is barely imaginable. The Master Builder is the pragmatic visionary, able to turn the most ambitious of dreams into reality.

It is potentially the most successful of all numbers in that it has hidden within it the inspirational insights of the ELEVEN, combined with the practicality and methodical nature of the FOUR, and the gentleness and femininity of the TWO.

If you are a TWENTY-TWO then you probably think of yourself as something of a walking contradiction. You own the ability to dream big, think big, plan big and, when you really believe in something or someone, you will find that you also possess enormous self-confidence, inner strength and belief that what you desire will manifest. Logical yet creative, profoundly practical yet visionary, you have a unique ability to see castles in the air and then *to bring the dream down from the Universe,* gathering the correct building materials together to start building the castle on solid earth and thereby making it a reality.

When in your full power, you have the power to turn the most ambitious of plans into success stories, and so you can inspire others with how common sense and practical insights can build anything, one brick at a time.

But then, on the other hand, you also sometimes doubt yourself or your abilities, and so run the risk of dreaming big, but not having the courage or self-discipline to make it a reality. You run the danger of being crippled by your own doubt and insecurity. It's a bit like owning the most incredible racing horse, entering him into the million-pound sweepstake at Ascot - and then not allowing your prize horse to get out of the starting gate, so he doesn't even have a chance of winning.

Most of us long deep down to create something or introduce something to the world that can change life for the better, that will have a strong positive impact on people's lives. You have that need too, to be worthwhile and purpose driven, but in your case, you have the ability to manifest it. People generally like working with you, because you can be an inspiring leader, because you have strong visions of lasting value, because you can be practical, pragmatic and down-to-earth.

In love you can be just as expansive. You desire the full love story, with the promise of romance, beautiful music and angels singing, and want others to experience it too. You will court the object of your desire with flourish and flair; when you pour on the charm, you are simply too hard to resist. You want the big wedding, the lavish honeymoon, the big engagement ring, and all the trappings of love, beauty and success. Once you have achieved the object of your desire however, be careful you don't become too practical and logical, or too disciplined and restrictive in how you think the love should progress.

Sometimes controlling, sometimes arrogant and superior, sometimes charming, sometimes inspiring, sometimes a visionary leader, sometimes swept away on the tide of your own imagination. One thing is for sure… love, life and business with you is never boring or mundane and indeed, can become an adventure of epic proportions.

Reliable, consistent, respectable, you are a good family person, and a strong protector of family values and traditions. You can also be superbly financially successful, as long as you recognize that sometimes you are your biggest worst enemy. In other words, if you own the racehorse, then get out of your own way and LET IT RACE.

When you come right down to it, the TWENTY-TWO really wants the opportunity to share their vision, allowing others to make contributions, building and creating and manifesting dreams into reality.

Other attributes of the TWENTY-TWO energy:

Out of balance, the TWENTY-TWO energy is: Self-sabotaging, self-doubting and insecure, lacking in follow through and self-discipline, can get lost in the blue sky picture and forget to bring it into practical terms, risk takers, gambling on 'get rich schemes with no solid foundation'.

In balance, the TWENTY-TWO energy is: Idealistic, expansive, visionary, master-builder, governance and leadership of a country or state. Philanthropic, with the ability to inspire others possessing masses of common sense, intuitive, practical.

Personal Goals: Integration of your ability to see the big vision, and to bring it in practical reality.

Fears: Loss of stability, lack of foundation, being suffocated by routine, disillusionment.

Success can come from: Politician, business owner, lawyer, administrator, entrepreneur, mentor.

THIRTY-THREE: THE MASTER TEACHER

The number THIRTY-THREE symbolizes the principle of guidance. When expressed to its fullest potential, the THIRTY-THREE lacks all personal ambition, and instead focuses its considerable abilities toward the spiritual and holistic uplifting of mankind. This is shown in its determination to seek understanding and wisdom first, for the world to make sense within, before 'preaching salvation' to others.

This is a very rare number, and one of the hardest of all numbers to live up to. It has been said that it takes a lifetime to fully grow into this energy, and that THIRTY-THREEs find things get easier, that life makes more sense, and they get better at living with this energy and being all that they can be, as they get older. For this reason, the THIRTY-THREE in full force is extremely rare.

The THIRTY-THREE is a contradiction in many ways. It carries the willful, capricious, enlivening energy of the THREE, the visionary insight and sheer inspiration of the ELEVEN and the nurture and capability of the SIX. Three very different and conflicting energies all rolled into one. No wonder it takes a lifetime to get to grips with being a THIRTY-THREE!

The nurturer side of you is reliable, consistent, respectable and it makes you a good family person, a wonderful provider and a strong protector of family values and traditions. There are times when you can come across as compassionate, guiding and soothing. People know they can relax with you and often feel healed by being in your presence.

Honest, brave, self-disciplined, hardworking, intelligent, sincere, devoted - you are all of these things. When operating at your highest potential you have a need and determination to find out 'what is my truth?' and then to put this truth into action in the order you create around your life.

Sometimes exploring this concept of 'my truth' may mean moving half way across the world, or doing a complete 180° turnabout, changing careers a couple of times in your life; sometimes it might mean being a little less radical, asking you to explore things closer to home. One thing is for sure: you have a need to know, to understand, to comprehend life at its deepest levels, and this need will be a driving force inside of you, keeping you moving and restless and unable to put down roots until you reach a level of comprehension that answers those burning issues that keep you awake at night.

The world needs to make sense to you, and you can become incredibly frustrated when you cannot see a meaning or reason as to why things are the way they are, or why people act the way they do. If there is one thing you love, it is to help (manage?) others - at times through a compassionate look or gentle touch; at times through empowering and uplifting their emotions; and sometimes, by creating a system of structure, rules and imposing regulations designed to improve another's daily lives, if they seem incapable of doing so themselves.

Although your need to find a deeper wisdom or truth makes logical and rational sense to you, it can leave people around you floundering to understand what really makes you tick? When it seems that everyone in your space is settling down with the 2.2 children, and the house in the suburbs, many people simply can't understand why would you want to go to Timbuktu? "I mean, what is it that you hope to find out there?"

Of course, you are not sure of the answer to that question yourself which can leave you wondering whether you really are 'just smoking your socks', or whether this force that is driving you is ever going to find some relief.

In love you can be fierce, devoted, gentle, healing, expansive, loyal, passionate and self-sacrificing, intolerant and demanding, all at the same time. You hold onto love as an ideal, and it can be hard for others to match up to your high expectations.

You can become critical when disappointed, or withdraw into silence while you mull things over, until you can see the sense in it. You need to be careful not to make your disappointment into a sermon that gets preached too often. People will stop listening to you (which you hate), or worse, simply tune you out and ignore you, which will make you feel invisible and invalidated.

Self-sufficient to the point of being a loner, liberated of mind and thought, unique, truly independent, you are all of these things… yet deep down, you crave the companionship and togetherness that comes from a true union of hearts and minds. Your challenge is to let things flow, without trying to direct the outcome too rigidly… life is a process, not a destination.

Other attributes of the THIRTY-THREE energy:

Out of balance, the THIRTY-THREE energy is: A loner, conflicted, prone to preaching or assuming that they have the answer to life, love and everything else, a martyr, self-sacrificing.

In balance, the THIRTY-THREE energy is: Honest, disciplined, brave, Christ-like, healer, compassionate, blessing, teacher of teachers, inspired, honest, monk, courageous.

Personal Goals: Searching for the truth, for the meaning of life, love, the Universe, and EVERYTHING else!

Fears: Lack of resources and love.

Success can come from: Parent, educator, artist, doctor, teacher, ascetic, mentor, leading, politician, governor, management.

SECTION THREE

Calculating Your Personal Numerhythms

What your date of birth reveals about you

Each numerologist will have their favorite method of working and mine most definitely is the **date and time** of your birth.

As I pointed out earlier, our **name** is given to us, and so it carries an energy and a vibration that wraps itself around us like a cloak. In the beginning, the cloak is way too big for our tiny infant bodies, and we show really very little of the essence of who we are. We are socialized by the situations of our life to become, to think, to act, to behave, to walk and talk in the manner that we are shown. Our parents, our extended family of grandparents, aunts and uncles, our teachers and community leaders all respond to us, providing us with a role model of how to behave, until we grow up, full of programming and suggestions and subliminal training. Our name reflects the energy that we begin to resonate with, to echo, to take it on as our identity… until over time we become what we have been programmed to become.

Our **date of birth** on the other hand, signifies our first independent act on this planet. As we are born, as we take that first breath of air into our lungs, we breathe into our being an energy that carries the knowledge, power and vibration of that specific moment and day in time. As we exhale our first breath, we are breathing the essence of *who we are* back into the Universe.

It is for this reason that I prefer working with the date, time and location of birth. For me it carries the power and potential of *all that I can become*, coupled with the beauty and fullness of *all that I am right now* in this moment.

SO WHAT INFORMATION DOES IT CARRY?

As we saw in the previous section, by adding the Day plus the Month with the Year we reach what we call the Life Path.

using our example of the 3 September 1975:

As we have learnt, we further reduce the 34 by adding 3 + 4 = 7.

The Life Path is 7. This is the **gross value** that we look which describes the personality, the person that the world sees.

Think of it as the big picture view, providing insight at a macro level. It is the shape of your canvas, on which we can start to draw a picture of who you are. We sketch in the broad outline first, and then keep going adding in more and more elements and characteristics, until we get to paint in the more intricate and detailed brush strokes.

The day, the month and the year all provide color and texture to the picture, allowing us to see with great clarity all that you are.

If we add just the Day and the Month together, we reach a value that we call the Life Purpose, Soul Purpose or Dharmic Number.

Using our example of 3 September:

And then continuing to reduce the 12, by adding the 1 + 2 = 3. The Life Purpose (also called Soul Purpose or Dharmic Purpose) = 3

This number is made up of your talents, skills and abilities. It also indicates your Karmic Load and is colored by your parental influence on the one hand, and the deepest need or craving that you have *coupled together with* the key trigger to unlock and maximize all these unique skills and talents that you possess, on the other.

When we examine this number with full attention and detail we can start to see your Soul Purpose in life; what it is that you have been placed on this earth at this time, to achieve and do; what it is that will drive you forward as you strive to understand your internal world; and how to operate in the world around you

The day of our birth carries with it the Talents and Skills that we bring into this life with us. It reveals our natural abilities, our default passions and potential. Simply by looking at the patterns inherent within the day we are born, we can see where our natural skills, and abilities lie, and which area or industry we should explore for our careers.

It also is the number that indicates the karmic lessons we are here to learn in this life. We can see the influence of our parents here, and the impact of our early life experiences in shaping who we become in later life.

In our example of 3 September 1975:

Day of birth = 3

The Talents and Skills Number, plus the Karmic Lesson number = 3

The month we are born in reveals those factors that we need to be in place to trigger the skills and talents we inherently possess, in order to achieve their full potential. Some people may need safety and security as the vital ingredient which allows their talents to really express themselves. Others might need spiritual understanding, while still others might need freedom, or chaos, or independence. Your unique trigger that allows your talents to reach their highest level of expression is indicated by the month of your birth.

It also indicates that which we crave and need the most in our lives in order to feel whole and fulfilled. When it is there, it becomes a trigger to inspire us to achieve, to become all that we can become. When it is not there, it has the power to sabotage and trip us up, and it is for this reason that it is also known as the Sabotage Value. We intuitively know when we are lacking some resource or ingredient that prevents us from achieving happiness or success, but often we are not really sure what it is… and in searching for that which we crave the most, we sometimes end up becoming our own worst enemy.

Still using our example, 3 September 1975:

September is the NINTH month = 9.

The Trigger to unleash the skills and talents = 9. It is also is the Sabotage Value.

The year within which we are born mirrors the paradigm into which we have been born. It indicates the energy and vibration of the time, the attitude of the world around us during the time our mother was pregnant with us, and the time of our birth. The social fabric and understandings at the time of our birth provide a vital clue into the way our lives are shaped from an early age, and the person that we become.

For our example of the 3 September 1975:

The paradigm value is 22.

LIFE PATH

Your life path determines your natural tendencies, abilities, and attitude toward the world. It gives us a general overview into who you are.

Your life path is calculated by adding your **Day of Birth, Month of Birth and Year of Birth**, and continuing to add until a single digit is reached. Here is the snap-shot version to refresh your memory… for in-depth information, refer back to Section Two.

ONE

When the ONE energy is out of balance, it can become a wee bit stubborn, headstrong, egotistical, ambitious, sometimes bordering on the tyrannical. It can be arrogantly bossy when pushed to the limit. But on the plus side, it is also original, independent, unique, courageous, strong, creative, and extremely capable and self-sufficient.

TWO

In balance, the TWO energy represents all aspects of femininity and grace. This is the peace-maker, the diplomat, the one who is truly able to see all sides of the story. Nurturing, compassionate, caring and loving when feeling safe and secure, an out-of-balance TWO energy can become extremely sensitive and overly self-consciousness, fearful and hesitant, over-conscientiousness and always putting others first to the point they get walked all over. They can also be manipulative, resentful, critical, sarcastic.

THREE

Our THREEs are creative, social, easygoing, visionary, funny and humorous, energetic, spontaneous, enthusiastic, powerful imagination, versatile, optimistic and playful. All brilliantly upbeat energies, but sometimes that powerful imagination can be prone to hyperbole and exaggeration, lack of direction, unfinished projects, sensitivity to criticism, laziness and downright apathy.

FOUR

Prone to rigidity, too cautious with limited perspective, unwilling to try new things; boring, stuck in a rut or routine, inflexible, unwilling or unable to see another's point of view – all of these can describe the FOUR when out of balance or under pressure. In balance, however, the FOUR energy is able to focus and apply themselves to the matter in hand from beginning to end, making them absolutely brilliant at Getting Things Done. Our FOURs are determined, reliable, conscientious, practical, realistic, traditional, manager, capable, trustworthy, and balanced.

FIVE

Restlessness, procrastination, prone to activity with no direction, lack of follow through, addictive, drama queen, with a propensity to depression or feelings of apathy and lethargy: all these qualities are highly descriptive of a FIVE energy that is feeling hassled or agitated. But the glorious power of the FIVE manifests in its ability to be larger than life, expansive, free thinking and adventurous. FIVEs are sensual, generous, often with a dramatic flair and a huge dash of charismatic, dynamism that motivates, inspires and enthuses.

SIX

In balance, the SIX energy is the nurturer, the carer, the best friend who truly cares and supports those around him or her. Compassionate, just, fair, able to see both sides of the story, reliable, domesticated and highly responsible, someone who delivers on whatever he or she undertakes. The flip side of this is that they can become rigid, inflexible, intolerant, resentful, withdrawn, stifling, strict, severe, and prone to anxiety when life takes a turn down a road they hadn't anticipated.

SEVEN

Out of balance, the SEVEN energy is proud, narrow-minded, distant, rigid, overly connected to the past, argumentative, exploding into temper or lapsing into a deep silence, a perfectionist, a loner. Their full power lies in their ability to search for truth and meaning, to analyze and assess, with full clarity and efficiency; they have huge powers for mental understanding. A seeker of truth, a specialist, inventor, thoughtful, spiritual, seeking perfection within themselves and those around them, becoming judgmental and critical when they or others fall short of sometimes impossibly high standards.

EIGHT

Decisive, courageous, focused, able to delegate and manage a project from its inception through to its final completion. EIGHT energy exudes professionalism and strength. They are often money orientated, able to solve problems and find solutions for anything and, as if that is not enough, they are also generally amazing at organizing anything - from the proverbial piss up in a brewery, to the Presidential Electoral Campaign. They can also however become belligerent, manipulative, angry, judgmental, stubborn, dictatorial, and overly materialistic when out of their comfort zone.

NINE

The true "old soul" one who possesses understanding, sensitive to those around them and their needs and desires. NINE energy is multi-talented, a great teacher. It is the humanitarian, the healer, the soul artist. It runs the risk however of losing focus or drifting aimlessly, becoming intolerant of others and the way they do things and, left without stimulation or purpose, can get into bad or self-destructive habits

ELEVEN

Out of balance, the ELEVEN energy is prone to self-illusion (delusion?) or self-deception, isolation, over-stimulation, and anxiety. In their element however, the ELEVEN energy is able to inspire, delighting in revealing higher truths to those around them in order to truly help people transform. It is poetic interpretation at its best, seeing beauty everywhere, idealistically romantic. It can also be the artist, celebrity, highly energized, psychological, radical, sensitive, idealist

TWENTY-TWO

The TWENTY-TWO energy craves opportunity to share their vision for a better life with others. It is truly participatory, allowing others to make contributions, with the power to build, create and manifest dreams into reality. It is also idealistic and expansive. This is the Master-Builder with the ability to inspire others while still holding onto masses of common sense,

intuitive, practical

THIRTY-THREE

A loner, often conflicted, prone to preaching or assuming that they have the answer to life, love and everything else, a martyr, self-sacrificing: these are some of the worst traits of the THIRTY-THREE. But wow, in balance, this Master Number is supremely honest, disciplined, brave and courageous, a healer, compassionate, a teacher of teachers.

Did you find that your life path number described the general you, but didn't *quite* get all of who you are? This is one of the reasons why in numerology it is important to read the person from all levels, in order to truly get to grips with who they are, how they behave, and why they will respond to one situation in one way but will respond completely differently under other circumstances.

In order to remind me that we are complex creatures with many different facets to our personality and persona, I like to keep the following diagram handy whenever I do a Numerhthyms analysis.

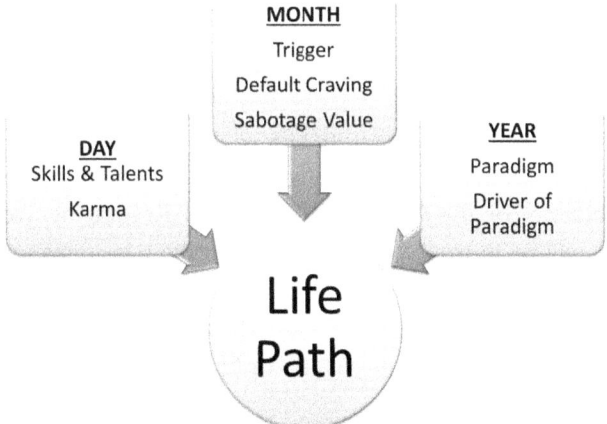

As I go through each aspect of the numbers, for example, the day, the month, or the year of birth, I jot down the key points that stand out to me. If you look at this diagram, you start to really understand that the Life Path only reflects the gross value of who we are.

SKILLS & TALENTS, KARMIC LESSONS

The **DAY** of your birth gives us an incredibly intimate insight into where your skills and abilities lie and what type of talents and gifts you will have an inherent, almost intuitive, understanding of. We can look here to see the interests, passions and capabilities that you uniquely possess. By understanding this number, we can see what type of career you are likely to excel at as well as the responsibilities and obligations you will naturally assume not only at work but also in your own home and personal life, with friends and family.

It is this number we look at to understand whether you will be a whizz at organizing and managing events (whether that be the annual family Christmas holiday, or the Company President's Round the World trip), or whether you will be more likely to be found in the basement sorting out the accounts and getting the household budgets ready for the tax-man. We can see if you are the unsung Domestic Goddess, or have the talent (and self-confidence) to be the next Johnny Depp or Charlise Theron.

It's all in the **DAY of your Birth**, and is calculated by adding the digits of just this day together to reach one single number. In the example we have been using, 3 September 1975, we would work only with the number 3. If you were born on a day with a double digit, you would add those digits together until you reach a single digit. For instance, if you were born on the 26th of the month, you would add up 2 + 6 to give you a value of 8 for your skills and talents number.

We will also look at this value to see the Karmic Lesson we are meant to learn and understand. In life, we often find that we are surrounded by the same type of experience again and again, until we either 'get it and get over it' or it gets the better of us.

One woman might find herself repeatedly facing episodes of jealousy and insecurity until she learns that self-worth and self-esteem is something only she can give herself; a man who refuses to be a leader might find himself in repeated clashes with authority until he accepts that he really is a strong leader in his own right.

Quick navigation links

If your Skills and Talents is a ONE, continue on page 74

If your Skills and Talents is a TWO, continue on page 75

If your Skills and Talents is a THREE, continue on page 77

If your Skills and Talents is a FOUR, continue on page 78

If your Skills and Talents is a FIVE, continue on page 80

If your Skills and Talents is a SIX, continue on page 82

If your Skills and Talents is a SEVEN, continue on page 84

If your Skills and Talents is a EIGHT, continue on page 85

If your Skills and Talents is a NINE, continue on page 88

If your Skills and Talents is a ELEVEN, continue on page 90

If your Skills and Talents is a TWENTY-TWO continue on page 91

ONE: Initiator, Leader, Director

Don't be content with just being a potato peeler! With your ability to lead, focus and think creatively, you should be planning the menu, running the kitchen, organizing the social events, doing the advertising and marketing, writing the website, and then dressing up in your glad-rags to meet, greet and network, all the while sparkling, captivating and inspiring others with your brilliant dazzle.

In short, you have the ability to be a fabulous all-rounder, someone who can apply logic and rationality when needed, but also with the capability of lateral thought. Wildly creative when you allow yourself to be, you are also able to take a deep breath and launch yourself off the diving board into the pool below, which makes you a very rare bird indeed.

When you are in a good space, you are amazing. Able to inspire and motivate, you can see a logical flow to how things get done, and when YOU are inspired and enthusiastic over a project, you can quite literally move mountains. Strong, powerful and committed to delivering what you have promised on make you an ideal manager, project manager, leader, organizer and authority figure.

Sounds fantastic doesn't it? Of course, the key phrase here is 'when YOU are inspired and enthused'. When you are not convinced of the project's success, or that it's something that you really want to be involved with, you can become hard to motivate, hard to excite, strong and stubbornly intractable in your disapproval, non-commitment and non-action. While non-action for others might simply cause lethargy, with you it can be destructive and cause depression, irritability and deep unhappiness. Your energy was meant to move, to be active, to reach and strive and to lead.

You retreat into being bossy and overbearing under pressure or when you have to deal with someone who you don't respect, or has no idea what they should be doing. Ironically, you hate being bossed around by others, and being told what to do by someone else (heck, *ANY*one else) can make you dig in your heels and refuse to play the game according to someone else's rules - even to the point of sabotaging the project. Non-delivery, non-performance and excuses drive you batty when you are in charge, but you need to be aware that you also have the very real tendency to do this to those who are 'in charge' over you, if you do not like them or the control they wield over you.

Your Karmic Lesson is to stand in your own power, and to *own all that you are*, without becoming pushy or giving into stroppy displays of temper when things don't quite pan out the way you wanted - or sinking into lethargy and non-action because you can't figure out how to overcome the next hurdle. You are strong, you are courageous, with the ability to be utterly original, independent, unique and in addition, you can be extremely capable and self-sufficient.

The strange thing is that although we encourage people to "be who they are" and "to stand in their own power", we don't really want them to do so because we find it too threatening, too intimidating to see how intoxicating we can be when we allow ourselves to be fully present within ourselves.

You may find that people around you don't like this, and will try to resist you, or ignore you, or prevent you from achieving. In the words of that great sporting company "JUST DO IT … anyway!"

TWO: Mediator, Counselor, Social Worker

We have already discovered that the TWO energy can be diplomatic and gentle, the meditator who is truly able to see all sides of the story. We know that in balance they are nurturing and compassionate, gentle and kind. Out of balance they can become emotional bullies, victims of their own sensitivity and heightened self-consciousness, and can find themselves becoming paralyzed by self-doubt, becoming a non-starter / non-finisher in the process, as they give in to their own insecurities and inner fears.

A classic TWO cycle is to give, give, and then give some more, as this energy really does want to help and assist and take care of others. However, if they feel under-appreciated or unsung a little too often, they can become resentful and manipulative, sabotaging with words and passive aggressiveness, until they feel guilty about not giving enough, or seeing others do what they feel they should be doing. They then dive headlong into giving and giving and giving some more until they feel resentful again; and the whole cycle repeats itself in a never ending ritual of giving and resentment.

The danger for our TWOs is that they are often far more concerned with what people think of them than with what they think of themselves. Because they are always trying to be helpful and kind, they run the risk of becoming the voluntary slave, the doormat, the Cinderella who gets left behind while everyone else dolls up for the Prince's Ball. TWOs get a real kick out of being needed and wanted, and so in a 'if I do everything for you, you'll want me even more' kind of logic, they are big on over-commitment and under-delivery, letting commitments drop, leaving unfinished business scattered in their wake, and generally dropping out of things at the last minute because they feel too sensitive, too tired, or too lacking in energy to continue.

Part of the Karmic Lesson for the TWO is to commit completely to the task at hand, to be self-referred and less 'other people' referred, and to finish what they start, no matter what it takes.

The rest of the Karmic journey? Because TWO thrives on relationships, this is where their work must take them. A relationship with a two rarely runs smoothly. Either they suppress and sublimate their own needs to feed their partner, doing whatever they can to make them happy until they wear themselves out with resentment and anger; or they have the potential to be so intent on not giving into anyone's else needs and desires that they become selfish and arrogant, demanding that others respect and acknowledge their self-worth, while all the time fighting it with all their might.

Insecurity, lack of self-worth, feelings of inadequacy plague the TWO until they come to a point where they allow themselves to truly find that point of self-referral, self-awareness and self-knowledge.

Ideal Careers if your skill and talent number is a TWO: working with people, human resources, mentoring, training, teaching, nursing, social worker.

THREE: Visionary, Creator, Inventor, Designer, Sales Person

Creative, social, easygoing, visionary, funny and humorous, energetic, spontaneous, enthusiastic, powerful imagination, versatile, optimistic, playful, - all of these describe the THREE talent in its balanced form. Out of balance? Sometimes that powerful imagination can be prone to hyperbole and exaggeration, lack of direction, unfinished projects, pie-in-the-sky thinking, sensitivity to criticism, laziness and downright apathy.

THREEs love to create, to bring new creations into being, to breathe new life and watch that life take form. THREEs quite literally are pregnant with possibility, with potential, with power. They are able to conceive new ideas and new ways of doing something, quite simply because they are non-traditional thinkers. They always seem to see things from a different angle, from a different perspective and it is as if that ability to stand apart from traditional belief allows them to see the possibility of opportunities cascading into reality.

In a brainstorming situation, you want THREEs to cluster around the table because they will kick all possibilities up for consideration. The THREE needs to learn the patience, however, to be able to nurture these possibilities or to follow through into completion in order to bring that idea into manifestation. Because they can be so consumed with the amazing 'fantasticness' of the idea, they can burn up with excitement at the thought of all it can achieve - and burn themselves out just by talking about it, leaving no energy left for actually getting it done. If there was one thing the THREE energy needs to learn it would be that talk is cheap, and discipline often achieves what brilliant ideas seldom can on their own.

The THREE energy manifests its skills and talents with charm, vivaciousness and an almost magnetic quality that immediately endears (ensnares?) you. Their enthusiasm and excitement can be overpoweringly contagious. The THREE in its full unharnessed power sees no obstacle or barrier as too hard to penetrate. Everything is do-able, everything is achievable, everything is just 'going to fall into place'.

The problem comes in when the THREE realizes that things often don't just slot into place by themselves, and damned hard work is required. Constant commitment and re-affirmation of the vision is necessary. Responsibility and accountability are essential if success is to be found, no matter in what area the endeavor may be in: love, work, money, self-realization.

All too often, the THREE resorts to 'blue sky thinking' of all the things he will do/ is going to do /one day, when… without ever realizing that all he is doing is chasing the proverbial rainbow in never-never land.

When the promised pot of gold doesn't materialize, THREEs can become childish, lacking in accountability, becoming unable to make decisions or take a clear direction. They can blame others – or the situation, the politics, the global economy - for their non-achievement, becoming martyrs burnt at the stake of their own cause, instead of standing with power and clarity.

Therein lies the Karmic Lesson: The Karmic Power of the THREE is ABUNDANCE. Its power lies not just in creating but in COMPLETION. Unless the ability to nourish the idea comes from within, to nurture it to the point where it is able to not only breathe, but walk and talk and eat on its own, then true abundance can never be sustained.

FOUR: Builder, Balancer, Organizer, Routine and Order

Our FOURs have a remarkable ability to start a project at the beginning, work logically through it and most importantly of all, to *finish* it completely to the point that all the t's are crossed and the i's are dotted. They are superb in bringing order, routine and rules into systems and projects that need it.

Whether your skill is managing the books of the credit control department or the entire financial requirements for a multi-million dollar company; whether it is managing all the aspects of a building site or breaking a "blue sky" project into manageable, achievable bite sized chunks; or whether it is simply managing the various aspects of a domestic household - one thing is for sure. Things get done with you around and generally get done right the first time.

You are reliable, realistic, and methodically work through things until you have achieved what it is that you set out to do. It is this quality that makes you a gem in any office department, but if you are honest with yourself, there are times that you really get fed up with sorting out other people's messes so *they* can go out to office party while *you* stay at your desk late every evening burning the midnight oil.

Being the salt of the earth, that all important cog that keeps the office running smoothly or the backbone of the family, is all very well and fine but you can get so tied up (and tired out) with keeping things running like clockwork (whether it is the finances or the annual family holiday) that others very quickly learn that they never really have to think very much, or actually do much of anything, with you around. You simply step up and set to, getting things done, because you feel deep inside that 'it's easier all round if I just get on with it'.

FOURs have a keen sense of what is fair or unfair, right or wrong, just or unjust. Because they crave balance and security of the known and familiar, they often stay in situations long after they have become toxic or destructive, simply because the familiar becomes a comfort zone.

Your Karmic Lesson is to find what it is in life that makes you safe and secure on *all* levels - remember that you are not just a physical being but that you also have emotional, mental and spiritual aspects as well. Each facet of you needs to feel safety and security in order to thrive.

Do not simply give into routine and law and order, or mistake the illusion of a comfort zone for true safety and security. Sometimes comfort zones are simply a well-padded jail cell. The danger for the FOUR is that this can make you inflexible, unwilling, rigid, intolerant and narrow-minded in the process. While the material world holds the illusion of making us 'feel' safe, with the creature comforts of home, money, job, when we sell our SELF out to achieve safety on the physical, then we need to ask if we are compromising our emotional, mental and spiritual safety in the process. If the answer is yes, it can cause crippling bouts of non-specified anxiety or depression.

FIVE: Motivator, Persuader, Change Agent, Communicator

The FIVE Energy holds the ability to spur (and yes, it must be said) to provoke people to deep thought, stimulate interest and attention, and change the status-quo of those around them.

If the FIVE energy describes your talents and skills number then you know that you have an energy that people either love, adore and absolutely understand… or on the completely opposite end of the spectrum, where they just don't get you at all. You can be loving and compassionate, caring and kind, but sometimes when the words come out of your mouth they seem to provoke people instead of pacifying them. Sensitive, sometimes hyper-sensitive to an absolute fault, the FIVE can become arrogant, critical, scathing and brash when she feels hurt or vulnerable. Her words can sometimes become verbal missiles which can wound others deeply, as she deflects anticipated pain in what can come over as an 'get them before they get you' attack to her partners and friends.

FIVEs feel powerfully about things that matter, and often get drawn to causes or projects that smack of social or environmental responsibility, becoming outraged (at its extreme level) or confused (in milder forms) by the apathy of others who just don't seem to care about the 'important' things in life.

As a FIVE, whenever you feel strongly about something, you have the ability to bring enormous passion, conviction and commitment to the project at hand, whether that is teaching a reading programme to kids in the Bronx, raising sponsorship money for a destitute village in Africa, saving the whales or running for government office in some political race.

One of your key phrases could be 'I want my life and work to stand for something, I want to have made a difference in this world' – and as long as you can see that your work and your effort is making a discernible difference on some level to someone, you will continue with passion and intensity, putting in incredibly long hours, enormous perseverance and endurance, and total dedication to achieving the cause.

The FIVE as a skill and talent indicates that you will have a driving need to establish your reality physically, which on one side of the spectrum can manifest itself with great passion for sport, body consciousness and sensuality. The body needs to move, to be active, to be fed, to be stimulated, and you will feel confined and restricted if you are unable to do so. A fantastic stress release for the FIVE skill and talent would be to go on a gruelling hike or run along the river.

Life just seems to make more sense when seen through the realm of the physical senses, which can become almost addictive. Of course, the other end of the spectrum is equally as likely, where we can also see the FIVE just as likely to establish their physical reality not with body consciousness, but with the satisfying of the sensual – instead of feeding the body with exercise, it is just as possible to feed the body with food, drink, drugs, all of which are toxic and destructive in their own way.

The Karmic Lesson for the FIVE is to realize that *she alone* holds the choice of the direction she will walk in this life. Yes, we are all products of our childhood, yes of course we are all affected by our parents, school, relationships and the early experiences of our lives, but we have to reach a point where we either consciously choose to be bigger than our past or to continue to perpetuate it. The FIVE needs to recognise that *who she chooses to be, act and believe as an adult is a conscious decision*, not a subconscious programmed response to previous hurts or programming of her childhood. When she gets that truth, *really truly gets it*, then she will be powerful beyond belief.

FIVEs stand at a point between heaven and hell. She chooses (sometimes blindly it is true, but she still chooses) what it is she will manifest… because ultimately, manifestation is what the FIVE is all about. Wherever she puts her attention, her passion, her energy, her power, that is what she will create. It's hard to accept that 'my life is the way it is because I have made it so' when things are going to hell, but therein lays the gift. If I can recognize that I am here because of my own actions *and* non-actions, my own decisions *and* non-decisions, my own words *and* non-spoken words; if I can own that truly we create our own tomorrows; if I can harness these truths with all their unlimited power, then there truly is no limit to what I can manifest in my life and in the lives of those around me, in the community, in the world.

When the FIVE gets this truth, *really gets it*, she becomes the Change Agent the she was born to be.

SIX: Nurturer, Home Builder, Healer, Best Friend

As we tune into the SIX energy, we see the energies of the carer in action. People who are born with the SIX as their Skills and Talents number often end up carrying responsibility and obligation - just as a pack horse carries enormous loads over long distances without the opportunity of ever putting the weight down. By the time the pack horse gets to its destination and is unloaded, it has forgotten how to skip and dance and frolic. Instead it has become responsible and reliable, and meekly waits to be loaded (and overloaded) for the return trip down the mountain side again.

People with this energy are often known as the 'perfect corporate employee'. Why? Because the SIX picks up unfinished threads, and weaves them together until they make sense. The SIX struggles to leave anything left unfinished and so, even as everyone else is charging out the door eagerly looking forward to sundowners and gossip at the end of the workday, the SIX is rolling up his sleeves and preparing to step in and sort out, fix up, take care of and finish what others have left undone.

This is not to be confused with workaholic tendencies mind you. The SIX can no more walk away from a job half done than a THREE can stop herself from dancing through a field of daisies.

Add to this the need to take care of everyone and everything, to keep things working in a harmonious flow, to avoid conflict and stress, the tendency to put the needs of others first (maybe not all the time, but certainly most of the time) and you get an energy that, like the proverbial candle, can burn itself out at both ends.

Make the SIX feel safe and you will have a best friend for life, loyal to the point of devotion. Stress her out, and you will feel the shutter doors clanging shut. The SIX retreats within when she feels pressurized or vulnerable, becoming inflexible, rigid, stern, and resentful… and yes, let it be said, sometimes downright bossy.

'Comfort and safety' are two words that allow the SIX to flourish, but don't make the mistake of thinking that they don't take risks or are not able to think outside the box. SIXs are superb in fact from this perspective, because they have such a keen sense of what needs to be done, are acutely aware of the 'when and how' of things - and they also have a rather unique ability to dot every i and cross every t, to ensure that things actually happen!

So what is the Karmic Lesson of the SIX? That responsibility and accountability is an INDIVIDUAL undertaking. Sure, you can lay the frame work, do the work, motivate and explain, create all the opportunities… but as the old adage goes, you can lead a horse to water, but you cannot make him drink. Just as you cannot drink for someone else, you need to internalize that you are not accountable for someone else's actions, thoughts, behaviors, achievements (or non-achievements). There will be times where there is nothing that you can do to 'make things better'. Each person has to choose and act on that desire themselves.

At times all we can do is be a witness and **not** take on the obligation and responsibility of others.

Your need to help and look after and take care of others is admirable to say the least. But the guilt and the pressure that you sometimes place on yourself to be the carer and nurturer on every level is truly your trap, not least because it keeps you from helping, nurturing and growing yourself.

Susan Schöning

SEVEN: Analytical, Specialist, Seeker of Truth, Detective

If ever there was contradiction in terms, the SEVEN skills and talents screams it out loud. The SEVEN is the most remarkable of all the energies from a skills and talents perspective, because it has the ability to specialize and excel at anything it puts its mind to.

SEVENs own that ability to naturally enter 'the zone', that magical place where effort becomes effortless, where accomplishment comes naturally, where excellence is par for the course. When we talk of the super sportsman who is able to tune out the world and just zone in on the sweet spot, or the super business man who is able to turn every deal into gold by narrowing his focus only to the matter at hand, or the mystical seeker who can shut out the world in his single minded pursuit of the Divine Mysteries, we are talking of incredible, mesmerizing SEVEN quality in action.

You might scream and shout for his attention until you are blue in the face but if your man is 'in the zone' of narrowed focus and exclusive attention, he will barely notice you until he has achieved what he needs to achieve. Emerging from this super-specialized tunnel vision, he might blink up at an image of you glowering and snarling at him and ask 'what's made you so angry?'

This ability to hone in to the matter at hand, to exclude any extraneous details, to sift out the superfluous and focus only on what is vitally important in this moment is both a blessing and a double edged sword.

The very process of specializing brings with it a harsh companion - the intolerant pursuit of perfection, focusing to the exclusion of all else. SEVENs can experience extreme loneliness; a point where he finally raises his head only to discover that the rest of the family has gotten really tired of waiting for him to finish his 'important things' and realize that they are also important. Also, this ability to analyze and assess the situation succinctly can plunge the SEVEN energy headlong into suspicion and paranoia, consuming him relentlessly as he analyses and assesses down to the minutest micro-level.

Like with any number, the SEVEN power can be turned inwards where, because it is so analytical, so seeking of perfection, so tuned into specialization, these qualities begin to almost cannibalize and consume, leaving behind pride, arrogance and narrow mindedness (as opposed to narrow focus). This in turn can lead to: Mood swings, emotional manipulation, intolerance, judgment, criticism, distantly hard to please, with impossibly high standards, for themselves as well as others.

These high standards are so well… high and so damned hard to reach that sometimes the SEVEN dooms himself to failure before he even starts. If the SEVEN doesn't think something is going to work, he won't even put himself out to try. Unless the SEVEN is completely, totally convinced of success, it's hard to even motivate him to get out of bed in the morning, and apathy and dejection follow rapidly.

The Karmic Understanding for the SEVEN is to find their own center, their own pivot. In order to do so, they will have to go on a sacred journey of discovering and recognizing what their skills and talents are, and allowing themselves to honor them – without arrogance, without bragging, without false humility or pride, without sublimation.

The Karmic Lesson is to learn to be self-referred, to be aware and cognizant of its own power, simply because it is an unassailable fact of life.

The SEVEN runs the risk of their ego leading them, insatiably demanding recognition and approval from others. When public approval comes, the ego is fed, and they feel capable and strong; but what happens when public approval doesn't come – or worse, your public is downright disapproving? When the ego is in control, the identity of the SEVEN is fed from others, which means that the SEVEN cannot ever find his or her way into the 'zone'. In order to get into that magic place, you need to be able to detach from what the rest of the world says, tune into your own center, and enter into the sacred portal alone.

EIGHT: Control, Delegator, Manager, Professional, Judge

We have heard that the EIGHT Energy is decisive, courageous, focused, able to delegate and manage from the beginning of a project through to its final completion - and all of this is especially true for the person who has a Skills and Talents EIGHT energy. There is strength in this number. It holds the power to get things done, to commit the resources to whatever project is required and to see things through to completion.

People with an EIGHT as their day of birth are quite literally survivors and thrivers in the world. Somehow, they intuitively seem to understand the parameters of the Game of Life, and are able to make their way through it (albeit battered and bruised somewhat!) no matter how hard, how uncomfortable, how high the obstacles seem to be.

They have an ability to put their shoulder to the wheel, to exert their not inconsiderable strength of mind and to get things done. Like their sister energy the FOUR, EIGHTs thrive on a regular balance and harmony and method to things, but are far more able to take risks. They can be spontaneous and are quite comfortable standing in the limelight, something our FOURs don't really enjoy. In fact if they are honest with themselves, EIGHTs thrive on recognition and approval, and sometimes yes, the more public the adulation and adoration, the better!

Most EIGHTs don't take anything for granted. Everything has a value, everything has a price, and everything needs to be negotiated. There is an implicit contract in everything: relationships, money, emotions, feelings, possessions, with an 'if I do this for you, what will you do in return' attitude that may seem mercenary and materialistic to some.

It isn't, however. It is far more profound, and much deeper than a mere materialistic keeping of scores. Rather it is an acute sense of obligation, responsibility, fairness, and awareness that causes the EIGHT to keep track of what has been received versus what has been given.

A common flaw of the EIGHT as a skill and talent energy is to give, copiously and generously, without ever being asked or expected to. They can't seem to help themselves from volunteering to step up into responsibility, committing themselves way over and beyond the call of duty. That isn't the flaw however. With their keen (sensitive?) state of fairness,

EIGHTs expect others to either recognize and value just how much they have given, or to commit at their level of commitment. When that doesn't happen, EIGHTs can feel a wee bit miffed, spiralling rapidly into resentment and the resulting 'I'm not going to play with you anymore' withdrawal causes hurt emotions and, in its extreme, broken relationships and severed friendships as they cut off all ties and connections to the person completely.

It is their weakest point really in an incredibly strong, powerful, efficacious energy and one that can cause them immense hurt and suffering.

An EIGHT will feel incredibly uncomfortable having been given something 'for nothing'. 'No such thing as a free lunch' is a key belief. They don't like to feel indebted to anyone or anything, and so keep a very balanced state of the account in their mind - whether it has been a financial exchange, a gift exchange or an emotional exchange. What this means of course, if you are dealing with an EIGHT energy, is that you can expect to be weighed and judged against this system of fairness and equal exchange.

The Karmic Lesson is to realize that this weighing and judging of themselves, and others, can be destructive when it is allowed into practically any relationship. People don't like to feel that they don't measure up. They don't like to feel inferior, criticized or compared to what 'should' or 'could' have been, and enter into resistance which then often forces the EIGHT into a show of superiority, criticism and aloofness: 'I'm right, and the sooner you realize it, the better off we all will be'.

Judging is always isolating, as its very nature demands that one person inhabits a position of superiority. Instead of judgment, perspective and discernment are the qualities that the EIGHT needs to attain, both within their own psyche, and in their relationships.

The EIGHT with discernment and perspective as their key qualities, is a rare gem of the highest value.

Susan Schöning

NINE: Humanitarian, Teacher, Soul Artist, Multi-talented

We call the NINE energy the "old soul, the one who possesses understanding" when it applies to either a Dharmic (Soul Purpose) or Life Number.

When it comes up though as a Skills and Talents number however, does this still apply? If this is your birth day number, you know that you probably have an aura that you project around you of being remarkable, capable, efficient, friendly, able to manage and excel at anything. You have an ability to appear to others as multi-talented, and quite capable of achieving whatever it is you put your mind to. In fact, if you think about it, people often expect you to pull rabbits magically out of hats, to save sinking ships, to achieve the impossibly regularly… and that's just before breakfast time!

But what you are probably saying to yourself is this: 'How can people think this of me?' or more likely: 'What do they possibly see inside of me that makes them think that I can achieve anything remotely like that?'

Deep inside the very capable external shell of the NINE lies a highly sensitive soul, one who doubts herself, who is often riddled by insecurities and doubts, one who is not sure that she has ever got it quite right, and so seems to be constantly waiting for someone to blow the whistle, exposing her as a fraud.

You are deeply sensitive to the under-currents, to the nuances of communication, to the unspoken dialogues between people, and it can be both unsettling and insightful all at the same time. It can be both your biggest ally and your worst flaw, and many NINEs do whatever they can to swallow down their deep sensitivity and cover it with what they feel to be a thin veneer of capability and efficiency.'I must stop being so over-sensitive' is a common comment for a NINE.

Because they often have this conflict within them teetering between 'I am good and strong and capable' versus 'I don't know enough, or how can I even think of doing this', the NINE runs the risk of getting distracted and sidetracked easily, more by their own sensitivity and internal self-worth issues than by external factors. Wading in a sea of non-completion of abandoned thoughts and projects of course does nothing for that self-worth and self-esteem issue at all.

Because of this, NINEs run the risk however of losing focus or drifting aimlessly, being intolerant of others and the way they do things and, left without stimulation or purpose, can get into bad or self-destructive habits

The NINE energy stands as a number of completion and end of cycles, and when translated into a Skills and Talents space, often indicates that the person has to deal with loss in his or her life. Sometimes this means the physical loss of loved ones, sometimes it indicates loss of money, possessions, property, and sometimes loss of relationships.

The NINE energy, more than any other energy within the Numerhythms system, has to come to terms with loss and gain, with holding and letting go, with attachment and detachment, and therein lies the Karmic Lesson.

Possession doesn't make us safe, whether it be a property, a person or a place. In fact possession keeps us attached and bound, and held by others' will or desires.

The NINE will always, always, ALWAYS be faced with questions about 'Who am I, What am I, What do I believe?' In essence these are deep spiritual questions, pushing us on a quest for the meaning of life, the meaning of all life.

It is the number that feels most keenly the push for self-development, for spiritual and psychological understanding in all aspects of life, for the quest for personal self-realization (if not on a spiritual scale, then most certainly on the global human scale). Because of this inner drive, the NINE excels in mystical pursuits, in psychological and emotional understanding, in soul work… and whether she is employed as an estate agent or a credit controller, will always have this deeper throbbing inside her reminding her that surely, certainly, there is more life than this.

Susan Schöning

ELEVEN: Artist, Psychologist, Actor, Radical, Celebrity

I have heard it said that in some regions of Canada you can experience five seasons in one day. A Canadian friend of mine once told me that you can wake up to almost blizzard conditions, be baking in sweltering heat by mid-morning, get blown off your feet by a gale force wind in the afternoon, and then have a hail storm with stones the size of golf balls at night. Going outside to check on the damage caused by the gale-force wind and the hail stones, you can watch as the clouds begin to disappear before your eyes to reveal a starlit sky. It sure takes some getting used to, she says.

As a Skills and Talent number, ELEVENs are a little bit like the weather in Canada; tantalizing, charismatic, intense in one breath, depressed, uncertain, low self-esteem with the next, sparkling, effervescent and dynamic with the next, beautiful, soft and sensitive the next.

They can be the actress, the poet or the play-write with ease, able to step into any role that life throws at them, whether that be counseling and understanding others in the capacity of psychologist; inspiring and activating others as a radical activist; or as the celebrity who stands in the spotlight captivating and alluring.

Mercurial certainly. One could say they change their temperament like the weather! But it must also be said that they have the ability to transform themselves, those around them and their environment with one wave of their magic wand. Because magic is what these people possess, by the bucket load. Like the magicians in the famous Harry Potter series, they need to be trained and guided as to *how to use* this magic in order to bring out the absolute best in them and those around them, because left untamed it can flare up, consume and destroy.

ELEVENs sit on a very precarious see-saw where absolute mastery, creativity, excellence and artistry sits on the one side, competing with over-stimulation, anxiety, over-the-top, depression, agonizing self-despair sits on the other. The see-saw has to find the point of balance on the pivot between the two extremes, and this is the Karmic Challenge of the ELEVEN: to find the point of balance, not pulled apart by either extreme.

This means finding the balance of self-control, self-awareness, self-worth, self-understanding.

All of the numbers have to come face to face with themselves on this journey, but the ELEVEN energy can be confronted with such conflicting sides of life that they will sometimes wonder what is real. Only too often, the ELEVEN Skills and Talents number can feel that life is a coin which gets tossed by the outside world and whether it falls with heads or tails facing will affect their mood, their talents, their capabilities, and how they see themselves.

The ELEVEN needs to be able to see the beauty, the joy, the romance of love and life in all its glory, *without getting sucked into its self-absorbing madness*; and to understand himself, all his dark sides and fears, *without getting pulled down into the abyss*. For the ELEVEN, the hard unassailable realization must be: 'We are *all* our own worst enemy'. The monsters we fear the most are not 'out there', or hiding under the bed growling menacingly at us and waiting until we are unawares to pounce. No, the monsters we face are the ones we have brought into being all by ourselves.

In balance, once they have found that pivot that brings their see-saw into balance, the ELEVEN energy, just like Harry Potter, can defeat even the worst evil.

TWENTY-TWO: Architect, Master Builder, Visionary,

Courage, bravery, risk takers, expansive, spontaneous, practical and big picture dreamers, all at the same time.

The TWENTY-TWO energy harnesses all the magic and charisma of the ELEVEN, and multiplies it with all the sensitivity and caring, nurturing power of the TWO to create an energy that, in its balance, can be truly exceptional.

It is fast paced, needs to be constantly moving, experiencing, achieving, and becomes stifled and ultimately self-destructive when it feels trapped - whether that be by the situation, by people's expectations or life's circumstances.

In the words of that great Queen song, the TWENTY-TWO birthday number shouts out to the world 'I want to break free. I want to be ME.' It is a driving force pumping through the blood, and if you find yourself in a relationship with a TWENTY-TWO, be sure that you give them room to move, experience, challenge and taste all that life has to offer.

If ever there was a contradictory number energy, the TWENTY-TWO is it. All the power and charisma (and delusional capacity) of the ELEVEN together with all the nurture and the sensitivity (and the manipulation and emotional blackmailing capability) of the TWO make for a complex personality.

Like the ELEVEN, the TWENTY-TWO needs to find the pivot, the fulcrum on which life finds the balance, that which gives all activities meaning and purpose. One TWENTY-TWO I know finds her balancing point in being an air nurse in the Australian outback. She meets her need for freedom, adventure and expansiveness through her job. An emergency birth in one place, a logging accident in another, an outbreak of food poisoning on a remote sheep farm; she loves her job and also that by doing what she loves, she is able to bring balance to chaos, and restore order after an emergency.

Another fascinating and charismatic TWENTY-TWO I know employs her exceptional talents by producing and directing a fast paced weekly TV show, a job that takes her all over the country working hours and schedules that would make a team of grown men cry with exhaustion.

But it's not always adventure, adrenalin, and action stations. We are just as likely to see a TWENTY-TWO running the financial department of an international firm, with vision and tenacity, or planning a military maneuver, or architecting the plans for a new eco-village concept.

We call the TWENTY-TWO the Master Builder, the energy that craves to do something that improves the lives of others. That might be on a physical level (like my Australian nurse) caring for their health and sorting out their emergencies; on an emotional, mental and empowering level (like my TV producer friend); or, like the architect, planning a better living conditions for a group of people that can benefit both them and the environment.

Inspiring, certainly. But the one gift that sets the TWENTY-TWO apart from being pure pie-in-the-sky, castle-in-the-air thinkers and non-achievers, is that they come holding buckets of common sense, practical know-how, and a real desire to the get their hands dirty.

So, what is the Karmic Lesson of the TWENTY-TWO? TWENTY-TWOs are born, itching to get going. They are active (constantly active, if you ask their parents!) on the go, always challenging and being challenged. There is an absolute certainty that they have come to this planet at this time to do something BIG, something important. 'A small life is for everyone else, not for me!' the TWENTY-TWO might say - and because of this, they sometimes can appear a wee bit arrogant, a wee bit dismissive of others who seem content to settle for the white picket fence and 2.2 kids in suburbia.

The TWENTY-TWO needs to realize that everyone has to start somewhere, start small. Even the most important Guru has to be trained, has to submit to guidance and discipline before he could start his journey of changing the world… and so too, must this energy.

In order to change the world, you first have to understand it; in order to help improve the lives of others, you first have to live with them and understand what they really need, before you set about giving them a better life experience.

The TWENTY-TWO needs to be prepared to serve an apprenticeship, to learn about life, love and everything else. Of course, because they just want to get going, asking them to practice patience is like swearing the worst of all four letter words at them!

It's not an easy energy to carry when you are young, and if you are a twenty or thirty something TWENTY-TWO reading this you probably have experienced deep frustration and irritation about projects that haven't gone according to plan, people who fail to see your sincerity and passion (and let's face it, your genius), and a life that just hasn't slotted into the right holes yet.

But like a fine wine or even Balsamic Vinegar, the best taste comes from a bottle that has lain in the dust in a quiet dark cellar for a few years. Like that bottle of fine wine, you have all the ingredients and resources within you to do whatever it is you wish to do. As you grow older, and more used to your own energy, you will find that common sense, maturity and a practical world view add a sparkle to a truly outstanding person.

The karmic word for you, Mr. and Miss TWENTY-TWO? Patience. All things come to those who wait.

THIRTY-THREE

Of course, there won't be a 33 for skills and talents, as our days in the month only go up to 31!

TRIGGERS, SABOTAGE AND SHADOWS VALUES. DREAMS OF DEEPEST DESIRE.

It is the biggest irony in life that that which liberates us also has the ability to break us. That which we long for the most also contains the seed of our biggest fears in life. What we secretly dream for in the hidden depths of our being has the power to cause enormous conflict within us, as we walk along this journey called life.

Your trigger, your dreams of deepest desire and your sabotage value actually come down to the same thing, just seen from different sides. Each reveals a unique perspective of you, and how you respond to life. It's a bit like looking in one of those magic mirrors at the fairground. If you look from one angle your reflection becomes thin, skinny, impossibly long and stretched out, yet when you just move slightly forward or backwards, you are transformed into a short squat fat troll. You know it's still you, it still has the essence of you, but it becomes distorted depending on where you stand and how you look at the mirror.

We all have deep dreams, hidden desires and secret longings and yet in a cruel twist of fate, we are all held back from achieving and manifesting that which we long for the most.

It's a bit like realizing that the Holy Grail lies hidden at the back of a dark cave. To reach it though, we need to crawl through impossibly narrow tunnels in pitch blackness, with who-knows-what crawling or slithering around in the darkness. The prize is holding that Holy Grail in our hands, but the journey to get to it will bring us face to face with our darkest shadows.

It's a tough journey, and one that we humans spend as much time avoiding as much as we can. What if we face the darkness and find that the Holy Grail doesn't really exist? What if what we *think* we long for the most really doesn't make us happy or fulfilled? What if once we get it, we realize that we no longer want it? Worse, what if we have to change ourselves, or our beliefs in order to get what we want?

This core value asks what we really want… but it also tells us what we need to be prepared to do in order to make it happen. I call this value the Shadow Lands, because finding the Core means facing the Shadows of who we are.

This value is calculated by taking the digits of the month, adding them together until you reach a single digit: For instance, if you were born in the month of April, your Trigger, Sabotage Value and Dream of Deepest Desire would be a 4. Similarly if you were born in December, which is the 12th month, we would take the 1 and add it to the 2 to equal 3.

Those born during November would leave the digit as an 11, as it is a Master Number, and so has a value all of its own.

Quick navigation links

If your Trigger, Shadows and Sabotage Value is a ONE, continue on page 96

If your Trigger, Shadows and Sabotage Value is a TWO, continue on page 98

If your Trigger, Shadows and Sabotage Value is a THREE, continue on page 100

If your Trigger, Shadows and Sabotage Value is a FOUR, continue on page 103

If your Trigger, Shadows and Sabotage Value is a FIVE, continue on page 105

If your Trigger, Shadows and Sabotage Value is a SIX, continue on page 107

If your Trigger, Shadows and Sabotage Value is a SEVEN, continue on page 109

If your Trigger, Shadows and Sabotage Value is an EIGHT, continue on page 111

If your Trigger, Shadows and Sabotage Value is a NINE, continue on page 113

If your Trigger, Shadows and Sabotage Value is an ELEVEN, continue on page 115

ONE: Trigger and Sabotage Value

We know the ONE energy stands for independence of thought, individuality, uniqueness and standing apart from the crowd. The person who has ONE energy as their Trigger Value certainly has the potential to stand out from the crowd, to fly high across a neon painted sky. Ironically it is precisely this potential that scares them and holds them back. It is far easier, far more comfortable to be at one with the crowd; there is safety in numbers.

But in order to do their best work, in order to become all that they need to be, the ONE Trigger needs to be able to stand alone, stand apart, sometimes walking long distances on their own. They have to get used to their own company and become their own point of reference; to self-reward and self-validate; to be able to stand and listen to people, listen to the voices of the world, but still able to recognize their own counsel, their own wisdom, and to hear and follow their own voice.

It can be a very confusing, contradictory message for their loved ones. On the one hand, ONEs crave togetherness, partnership and companionship, to be included and accepted. On the other, they crave space and time to do their own work, follow their own passions, to withdraw far from the maddening crowd, to be able to shut the door and be in their own private little haven. Add into the mix their desire to be unique, to sparkle and dazzle, to be an individual, to be their own person, together with their fear of losing their identity and we have some really confusing territory! Just as one aspect of life falls into place the ONE trigger is asking themselves whether this is what they want, whether they are settling too soon, whether they are giving up themselves in the process.

After craving a solid relationship, a ONE trigger can push it away as soon as he gets it, claiming that he feels suffocated and trapped. After pursuing the high flying career in corporate finance, she can give it all up just as she is becoming successful because she feels unsung or unrecognized.

'Why isn't anything ever good enough?' cries the ONE trigger. 'Why can't I ever be satisfied with what I have?'

Graham was born on the 31st January, and is a Minister in a church. He leads his 'flock' well, guiding, advising, bring balance and harmony and order into their lives. He is constantly bringing new projects into being, from prison outreach-programmes to youth action plans, to relationship classes for married couples. He seems to be constantly active, constantly available and part of the vibrant community that he has built up.

And yet... he has recognized that he can only do this work of 'togetherness and partnership' if he protects himself and his own personal space. How does he do it? He has found the ideal retreat some hundred kilometers away from home, on a dry and dusty sheep farm in the middle of the Klein Karoo in South Africa. He works his diary so that he can escape every couple of months or so. He has learned that in order to do his best work, he needs to protect his alone time, to recharge his batteries, but also to allow himself to have downtime in order for his brain to be creative.

His wife has also got used to coming home in the middle of a particularly pressurized week to find a huge sign stuck on the refrigerator, 'Gone Fishing'.

Karen was born on the 3rd January and is an amazingly creative graphic designer. She finds working in a studio surrounded by other graphic artists too loud and distracting, and so has set up a little home studio at the back of her house, where she spends her time working on her assignments and projects. She only comes to the office to meet with clients, present her designs to the ad agency, or to discuss a new project requirement.

She has all the discipline and focus that the ONE energy brings which allows her to work alone and the highly creative energy of the THREE as her skills and talents number – but in order for her to truly harness it and allow it to manifest, she has learnt that she achieves her best work when left on her own.

TWO: Trigger and Sabotage Value

Supporting, caring, loving, empathetic, compassionate, collaborative, team player, manipulative, deceitful, sly, devious, nagging, sabotaging, shy, withdrawn, unsure, submissive: Two sides of the same coin. In balance the beautiful capabilities emerge, but when pushed or pressured the possibility of retreating into silence or descending into sabotaging behavior takes over.

The deepest desire of the TWO is for harmony, peace, no conflict. TWOs want happiness and contentedness to pour out little golden bubbles of bliss on everyone all around them. They want to feel true love, experience real romance complete with champagne, roses and glorious sunsets, as they listen to the baritone voice of a singing Venetian Gondolier on the Grand Canal. They want to believe that cupid is about to dart his arrow of love into them at any moment - and they want everyone to feel the same level of beauty and bliss as they do. They are not selfish; they truly want to share all that goodness and loving feelings with everyone!

As a dream, you have to admit that it's powerful, intoxicating even. After all, who wouldn't want that? But they can be derailed by this deep desire or dream of how love is supposed to be. Because they want nothing more than harmony and non-conflict, because they desire peace and beauty (not just in love, but in *ANY* relationship: work, family, friends) TWOs run the danger of suppressing themselves in order to keep the peace. A TWO often doesn't express fully what she needs to say, keeping it inside and unexpressed until she feels unheard, invisible or non-validated. Once this feeling is entrenched, the TWO is classic at avoidance; 'if I don't look at it, it doesn't exist and therefore cannot hurt me'. A hurt TWO trigger will often simply shut up shop, withdraw and pull away, and close in on herself, snarling at anyone who gets to close. The more impenetrable she can make herself, the less risk there is of being hurt.

When faced with an issue of conflict, the TWO is more likely to be the one to back down, more likely to acquiesce, more likely to give in. In an argument, the TWO will either walk away, all the time kicking herself of the things she should have said/ could have said/ would have said if her mind and mouth worked together quickly enough; or she will retreat into a nagging 'phonic loop' of previous slights, hurts and wounding from previous unresolved arguments and non-expressed hurts, becoming all the more scathing and sarcastic as she warms up into comfortable territory. Her arguments tend to be repetitive, saying the same things over and over, almost as if she is dredging up the same file out of the filing cabinet again and again, and re-reading them with vicious vehemence.

I have always thought that the comic strip of Hagar the Horrible encapsulates the essence of the TWO… not Hagar of course, but both his wife, Helga, and his trusty side kick whom he drags on endless conquests of pilfering and rampage.

Helga his wife runs the home, looks after his every need, tolerates her brutish rampaging husband, supports and enables his long absences from home and praises him for the trinkets that he brings home from his latest raid. She also manipulates him shamelessly to get him to do what she wants: dressing in the right clothes, eating with the correct silverware, drinking out of the appropriate goblet. She bullies him endlessly, nags at him ceaselessly, and then, just when you think she is being an absolute bitch, she capitulates to him in a fit of uncertainty and submissiveness.

Throughout all of it you actually side with Helga, the long suffering wife, and you can understand the range of emotions that she goes through in the comic strip. The point is that Hagar adores her, you know absolutely that he would be unable to do any of his pilfering and rampaging if he didn't have her at home stoking the home fires.

The twist in the tale of course is this: once Helga gets what she wants… her man, her home, the trinkets and rewards from his conquests overseas, the proof that even though he is off marauding on some distant isle that he is constantly thinking of her… she is safe, relaxed, and the goddess inside of her, the queen of her own domain emerges, allowing her to be all that she was born to be.

And what is that? Supportive, loving, encouraging, enabling, facilitating, empowering, allowing.

THREE: *Trigger and Sabotage Value*

People who are born with a THREE as their trigger are often fiery, fast paced, quick moving, quick thinking. Playful, endearing, sometimes child-like, always up for a good laugh, a visit to the playground or a melting ice-cream on a hot summer's day.

There is something immediately endearing and captivating about the THREE trigger energy. Perhaps it is their willingness to laugh, to be friendly, to be amiable, to enjoy. Perhaps it is their ability to be spontaneous, to do it today and not wait for tomorrow. The THREE trigger doesn't want to have to wait for a rainy day to do something. He wants to get moving, get going now. 'If something is worth doing, it's worth doing now, isn't it?' he asks with dancing eyes, raising a quirky eyebrow at you and grinning mischievously until you find yourself saying 'oh go on then!'

As a trigger, this glorious energy has the potential to be creative and on the go; they generally get on well with people and, because of their natural enthusiasm for life, they can be superb in motivating and inspiring others. If your trigger is THREE, you will know that you cannot stand to be in tight situations with no control or no way out. Boredom is not for you, and you don't suffer senseless routine easily either.

The THREE is that sacred child that comes from the union of the male energy of focus and direction, and the feminine energy of support and nurture. Within him, he holds the reins of both of these powers in his hands. The deepest desire of the THREE is to feel these powers like horses beneath his hands, to gallop with them in exhilaration as the winds of life blow through his hair, letting the horses take him wherever they want to go, screaming with the rawness of it all. But of course, out of this deep desire comes the first sabotaging value for the THREE. Sheer abandonment is intoxicating, overwhelming - and terrifying in the extreme. What if I lose all that I am as I throw caution to the winds?

While the THREE fears routine and boredom, he also fears getting lost in the labyrinth of his own intoxications more, and so he holds himself in a kind of half-way land between giving in and holding out, and achieving absolutely nothing in the process.

The THREE needs to overcome the fear of his own power, of his own creativity, and of course that is not easy. The fires of creativity can burn bright and illuminate and shine, but they can also burn up out of control consuming and devouring in a cannibalistic frenzy. It's a bit like asking how to harness the power of the sun without burning your hands off. How do you catch a star without blinding your eyes?

The second sabotaging value of the THREE trigger comes hand in hand with his child-like reaction to life. Yes, it is endearing, yes, it can lead to spontaneity, yes, it can allow him to jump off the high diving board, the one that no-one else has the courage to because it is so high - but sometimes like a child, he waits to be given permission to go and play and have a good time. There is vulnerability here that sometimes gets overlooked. There is fear of not being liked, fear of abandonment, fear of rejection, fear of not being quite good enough… and if that is allowed to flare up out of control, the THREE sabotages himself by shunning responsibility, not completing or finishing a project that he has started, leaving a mess of scattered building materials behind him. Like a child, he sometimes needs to be told to stop playing, or to play fair, to come out of the sand box and pick up all his toys and put them away, to go and get washed up in time for supper.

Yes, children have the ability to play and have fun. Yes, they are vibrant and often irresponsible. But children have also been scarred from being pushed into a corner wearing a dunce's cap for their inability to come up with the right answer at school. Many children were raised in that old Victorian ethic where children should be 'seen and not heard'. All of these aspects sit side by side within the THREE, and under the right provocation, all the faces of the child can show themselves.

It can be frustrating, for the THREE just as much as it is for the person involved with him. Inspiring, motivating, endearing, fun, shining, vibrant on the one hand. Insecure, vulnerable, scattered, lacking responsibility and accountability on the other.

What to do? Go back to that which you know, that which is your truth, and start small, building up your trust in yourself and your capabilities, one step at a time. Take baby steps. The THREE needs to find out where their own borders lie and, as is true of any journey, they need to find that out by themselves.

FOUR: *Trigger and Sabotage Value*

Born in April, I am a FOUR trigger, and so it is with great deal of intimacy that I can write this section.

I remember a long time ago, my then-teenager brother saving up all his money and buying a ticket to the UK, which was to be the starting leg of his 'explore the world' gap year. After he had brought his ticket he had something like 300$ left in his pocket, which he was convinced would be more than enough to get him started in London.

We all went to the airport to see him off, and there was Tony, with just the one backpack and a sleeping bag hanging off the end of it. With no fixed plan in mind beyond getting off the plane at Heathrow, he was dying for the adventure he was convinced was about to start (his skills and talents number is an 11!).

'But where are you going to sleep tonight? Surely you have at least planned your first week in London?' I asked him. 'I have a few names of some youth hostels in London, I'll probably start off there,' he replied.

I was truly horrified. It was completely alien to me that someone could just get on a plane in South Africa and get off in London with no knowledge of where he was going to sleep that night. He laughed at his 'safe predictable sister, who needs to take her teddy bear and personal pillow with her before she can fall asleep'. I panicked for days about whether he would survive on the other end of the world in a strange country, with no fixed place to sleep.

Of course he survived. He saw the world. He worked in a kibbutz in Israel, packed fish in Alaska, visited Samurai Warriors in Japan, worked in pubs in the UK,(he can't quite remember what he did in Holland, but he knew that he had been there because of the stamp in his passport!), and today I am filled with admiration and respect for a young man who even at that age knew that he could get out there and see the world and survive. I couldn't do it, even now, in my forties, as much as I might want to.

The FOUR trigger needs to know that she is safe, first and foremost, and that she has a roof over her head, food in the fridge and the right clothes to wear for each occasion. Safe for her means the comfort of knowing what is to be expected, and so predictable and routine, while stifling for other energies, are the soothing balm of peace for the FOUR trigger.

A FOUR energy needs to know where she is going to put her pillow that night, whether that place is the Carlton Ritz, a two up, two down row house in the suburbs, or a cardboard box in Homeless City under the bridge. As long as she has a place that she can call hers, no matter how temporary, she can breathe easy. It would be a big ask for a FOUR to get off a plane in a strange country with no guarantee of where she is going to sleep that night. Travel is great, but it's even better when there is a plan attached of where to eat, where to sleep and what to do.

Once her immediate physical safety requirements have been met, she then turns her attention to long term security - how will I pay for everything when I am 98 and ¾? Not knowing where the next pay check is coming from or whether she will still be able to feed the cats tomorrow is enough to put the FOUR trigger into a deep state of anxiety. Keep that pressure up with no sign of light at the end of the tunnel and she can plunge headlong into a lasting depression.

As a Sabotage Value, the risk is obvious. If the FOUR Trigger is able to achieve her best work when she feels safe and secure in every respect (meaning not just physical, but mental, emotional and spiritual safety of being), the Sabotage Value is that she delays taking action, delays becoming all that she can be, stops herself from exploring and experiencing and living because of her desperate, overwhelming need to feel safe.

If she feels emotionally unsafe in a situation, or feels uncomfortable or challenged by people, she just won't go back. If she feels intellectually inadequate, she just won't open up again. If she has risked and lost before, it will take an enormous amount to get her to open up again.

Her dreams of safety and balance, harmony and order, predictable outcomes and anticipated results both drives her and trips her up all at the same time. FOURs have been known to stay in destructive relationships or jobs long after the expiry date is obvious to others – not out of blind loyalty – but out of an overwhelming need to feel safe, first and foremost, and secondly, a deep seated conviction that they have to see through what they have started off.

As a compromise of course, it is short lived. Physical safety at the expense of emotional, mental and spiritual self is not safety at all. It is only when she begins to realize this that she begins to transcend the sabotaging energy of the FOUR, and move with self-power into that which brings her into the realm of safety and balance – ownership and commitment to her own mind, body, and spirit.

FIVE: Trigger and Sabotage Value

If the FOUR needs balance and safety in order to thrive, the FIVE needs freedom and expansiveness. Like the THREE, he needs room in which to play and explore but unlike the THREE he doesn't need anybody's permission to climb those mountains. It is enough that the mountain range exists at all. It's there and it needs to be climbed so what are we all waiting for? FIVEs need to move, to push their boundaries, need to be active. They need to understand the world in which they live, and do so by employing all their senses. They need to compete and boy do they like to win, to be better than everyone else. A FIVE trigger can be absolutely sensual, totally physical, totally sense driven… and of course, as we know, the world of the senses can be intoxicating, drugging the senses on every level.

FIVEs love good food, good wine, good music, good sex. In fact, all the creature comforts have the ability to make the FIVE energy purr with pleasure. A comfortable home with a fire blazing in the hearth will win you a friend, if not for life, then certainly until the end of winter! FIVEs often have wonderful voices for singing or speaking, love making music or moving their body as the rhythm of the melody washes over them, love weaving tales of fantasy and magic… and the bigger the audience, the better.

If the Trigger for the FIVE is mastery of their physical domain, it can also be their biggest downfall. Over-indulgence and hedonism, apathy and everything going to hell can be just as much a part of this makeup. What this means is that the FIVE trigger is just as likely to be a master of the body as its slave... and therein lays the difference between the Trigger or the Sabotage Value.

Probably the best way to illustrate the FIVE Trigger and Saboteur Value is to picture someone with the good angel perched on one shoulder, and the bad angel camped out on the other. The FIVE stands on the ground but has the ability to touch the gates of heaven with one hand, and the gates of hell in the other. It all comes down to active, conscious choice.

We all know that the balance of the physical is found in correct nutrition, moderate alcohol consumption, repetitive and stimulating exercise routines. Understanding of the physical world in which he lives and patrolling the borders with diligence is a vital skill that the FIVE energy needs to learn. The FIVE craves mastery of his physical environment and, if he uses his body to achieve that, is toned, honed and oh, so incredibly sexy. The flow of endorphins that come from exerting the body can be enormously addictive... plus, they know only too well that the opposite sex find a lean, mean body irresistible.

But, moderation and enjoyment in the here and now, beneficial nutrition and stimulation of the senses can quickly give way to extremism of either magnitude. A FIVE is just as likely to become the born again convert of the sports temple, boring everyone with their rude, constant good health, micro-managing everything that goes into their mouth, their weight, every aspect of their exercise regime, pushing the body to higher and higher peaks of physical perfection, as it is to become the complete sloth, lazing on the couch with a beer and a bowl of chips, burping at the Super-Bowl, and putting things off for tomorrow, or the next day, or even better the week after next. FIVEs excel at procrastination! It has the ability to be super toned and super slim, or super tubby and super addicted; whether that be to the exercise regime, the sensual pursuit of pleasure, to work, to money, or to the darker more sinister pleasures in life, of drugs, alcohol and sexual addictions.

The FIVE sabotages himself with his capacity for excess, and for not knowing when enough is enough. A key word the FIVE needs to learn is NO, but sadly, it doesn't seem to appear very often in their vocabulary. It should be employed regularly, as in: Would you like more wine, would you like another helping of desert, would you like to take a puff of this, will you work more hours than anyone else, will you jump off the bridge attached only to this little itty bitty cord? All together now… NO!

Because of this exuberant physical capability and sheer vitality and 'presence' that the FIVE holds, people assume that she is always in a good mood, always in control, always in emotional harmony with herself. The FIVE though is very good at plastering a smile on her face, acting up and performing despite how dreadfully insecure or uncertain she feels inside.

I seem to be surrounded by FIVE triggers in my life at the moment. One person allows herself to get walked all over by everyone else, working all hours that they ask her to, because she hasn't figured out how to say no to them; another is an absolute workaholic, who can work all day long for hours at a stretch and only realizes she hasn't eaten when her stomach starts to protest after a 12 hour day. She escapes the office by running, pounding kilometers under her feet, stopping only when she is dripping in sweat and mindless with pleasure from the endorphins. She is also as skinny as hell. Another teaches Tai Chi, uses her mastery over her body to teach others how to gain mastery over theirs.

The FIVE trigger can get lost in a physical world of their own making all too easily, without ever realizing the message of it all. Quite simply, it is to be the expert on all levels.

To speak and lead; to listen and empathize; to challenge and grow; to have pleasure and enjoy; to walk the road on earth without getting sucked into either the madness of heaven and hell.

SIX: Trigger and Sabotage Value

Like a bird, our SIXs are at their absolute best when they know they have a safe, strong nest to return home to at night after a hard day of worming, singing, soaring high on the thermals and twittering in the branches. SIXs need to have their family around them. This is a number that is much more settled and stronger with their family around them, than when they are travelling solo.

Domestic contentment is an essential for the SIX trigger, and one of their deepest cravings is to have a content, happy home life, preferably with their own children running around happily, and the extended family somewhere round the corner.

This craving has the ability to ground them, make them strong and give them the wings they need to soar the highest of heights they are capable of… or to break their wings cruelly and trap them in a cage where they can only dream of freedom. When domestic contentment becomes domestic abuse, the SIX wilts and dies little by little. Hysterics and drama is not part of this make-up, and too much volatile energy can leave them completely depleted and burnt out on every level.

Like their sister energy the FOURs, SIXs thrive on routine and discipline and, without it, can degenerate into scattered, unfocussed and non-achieving. Because of this, a lot of SIXs put in a battery of self-imposed rules and regulations, a little like a sergeant major, of what needs to be done or what is the right way of doing things. They can become quite intolerant of others (but mostly of themselves) when things don't happen according to plan. Control is a key word here, and the SIX is just as likely to end up being controlled by others' whims, as they are to be the control freak, bossing others around.

If the Trigger is emotional safety, and emotional belonging, then their Sabotage Value is the search for it, and how they compromise themselves (and sometime their values, their beliefs, their needs) in order to get it *and keep it*. Loyal, committed, honest, hardworking, the SIX will do anything to keep his nest safe, to the extent of building barricades and erecting borders to protect his home from the marauding hordes.

Have you ever watched a bird build a nest to try to impress the mate of his dreams? He will toil at it for hours and days, choosing the building material with care and deliberation, decorating with just the right twigs, leaves and nesting material, building her a veritable palace just so that she will come and live with him, be his love, and have his baby birds.

He sings his little heart out to her, asking her to just come along and look at what could be hers if she will only take him up on his offer. He hops around, like an over-eager estate agent, hoping she will think that the nest - and he - are the hottest properties in town.

She only has to say yes and go inside, to make him puff up his little chest with pride and sing out a song of exquisite beauty to the love of his life. But oh, what if she doesn't, if she doesn't? He will stand, bewildered, destroyed and bereft, just wishing the neighborhood cat would come along and put him out of his misery.

Of course the message for the SIX is obvious, but obvious clues are sometimes the hardest to see. Controlling the environment doesn't create safety, building barricades of fire against the outside world doesn't always keep the inside cave protected, and sometimes you need to accept that responsibility for domestic bliss is a two way thing between you and your partner to be shared. It is not *always* your responsibility, not *always* your job to create everything from scratch and keep the home fires burning single handedly; you might even find that by sharing the load you actually get what it is you really need and want - which when we come right down to it, is the fairy tale romance and the 'happily ever after until death us do part' marriage.

SEVEN: Trigger and Sabotage Value

"There has to be more to life than this" could be the constant refrain of the SEVEN trigger value. "I am meant for something special, something important, something powerful; not for me a small life with small dreams. I am meant to be larger than life, bigger than big. There is a special purpose to my life, and I will not rest until I find out what it is."

These people are driven by a throbbing, unrelenting desire to understand life, and why people are the way they are. There is an unrelenting craving to hold the keys to life's solutions in their hands.

They seem to be constantly searching for Pandora's Box, giving others around them the impression that they are never quite happy with what they have at the moment, which is actually quite true. SEVENs need the secrets of the kingdom in order to completely fulfill their lives.

More than anything, SEVENs want *to know*, convinced that in the knowing comes true power. This craving for knowledge can spur them onto a journey of the highest spiritual seeking at its one extreme, or take them along a road of suspicion, paranoia, secrets and spies on another.

This quest for knowledge can spur the SEVEN Trigger onto a single minded pursuit along their objective, whether that is uncovering the mysteries of the Universe or, in a paranoid moment of mistrust, sifting through the jacket pockets and credit cards slips, and digging through her husband's brief case after he has been away on a business trip.

The Trigger is the need for truth and knowledge and awareness, the craving to enter into the zone, that sacred place where all things become clear, and anything becomes possible. The Sabotage Value is this: the SEVEN can become so focused on their pursuit for truth that they a) believe that the truth as they see it is THE ONLY truth, and then b) with superiority and an almost condescending smugness try to convince and preach to others that they are the sole holders of this truth, with all the zealous fervor of the born-again convert, and then c) become disillusioned, dejected and depressed when others can't understand their perspective or truth (or to put it bluntly, aren't really that interested in it) which makes them disinterested and non-participatory. To be dismissed, ignored or not validated for what they believe has the ability to push the SEVEN over the edge, and they are capable of having fits of histrionics that can be quite spectacular. 'Incandescent with righteous anger' is a phrase that fits the SEVEN pushed that little bit too far!

What the SEVEN needs to understand is that TRUTH has many levels and many interpretations. What is true at one level is no longer true at another;

what is true for one person may not be applicable to another. While pursuing truth, SEVENs need to remember that there are different portals that one can walk through in order to find it. 'There are many rivers that lead to the same sea' is a Sufi saying that SEVENs would do well to remember. SEVENs need to practice the art of standing in anothers' shoes for a while, to understand that there are different perspectives and viewpoints, and that it is ok for someone else to believe or see things differently. In fact, it might even give them a broader grasp of what is fundamentally true.

Single minded focus is wonderful, but sometimes the SEVEN needs to be realistic about practical matters. It is all very well and fine writing the best seller novel, but remember you can't just give up the day job (which pays for mundane things like monthly bills) while you follow your dream. Being the yoga teacher might be the true passion of your life, but don't walk away from everything that allows you to eat three meals a day while you are setting it up. History has been full of starving poets and artists. Yes, you have the focus and presence of mind to follow the passion, but stay practical and keep your feet on the ground at the same time.

EIGHT: *Trigger and Sabotage Value*

One of the things that the EIGHT Trigger possesses first and foremost is the ability to see things from many different perspectives, and not just from their own. They are truly able to stand outside of their own feelings, put their own experiences to one side, and look long and hard at the situation from all sides. 'What made you think about things that way?' could be one of their questions; although it must be said, that some EIGHTs are more likely to phrase that question like the chorus from one of my favorite songs by The Parlatones: "What the hell were you thinking? Were you thinking at all? What the hell did you believe you'd achieve?"!!!

Most EIGHTs are very fair, and operate to a very strict rule book of what is right and what is wrong. This means however, that in order to do so, they need to appoint themselves Judge and Jury over *what is right and what is wrong*.

As long as they can remain impartial and objective, they are able to judge with impartiality and perspective, adjudicating the situation with a keen sense of clarity. This is when we see the EIGHT energy in is full power: Solomon-Wise, understanding, fully getting the intricacies of the matter at hand, and being able to see the clear road forward for all parties concerned. The EIGHT hates to see injustice and cruelty at any level. Whether it is abused children, cruelty to animals or abuse in the work place, it is still abuse, and the EIGHT will stand and fight for the underdog, simply because someone needs to. Somebody has to fight for those who cannot fight for themselves, and this is something the EIGHT does with passion, vigor and determination.

The EIGHT Trigger has a loud voice, and he can use it to defend, explain, teach and encourage - or conversely, to obstruct, refuse, demand or deny. If he is on your side, then you can breathe easy; if not, the EIGHT is really superb at creating and causing trouble for those he believes have crossed him.

It is a quality that makes them loved and adored, or feared and hated. There seems to be no middle road with the EIGHT trigger.

However, this very pursuit of justice can trip them into their first Saboteur role and, if they are not careful, they are able to tip headlong into condemnation and criticism, stepping effortlessly into the executioner or hired assassin's shoes as well. The EIGHT needs to take care that they don't become the moral vigilante, simply to satisfy their own form of justice.

EIGHTs are superb at handing out criticism and judgment – but absolutely lousy at receiving it and, like a child, will fling blame, accusations, excuses and sarcasm at anyone who dares to suggest that they might be at fault. They are very keen on sticking to the rule book when it comes to judging others, but sometimes feel that the rules just don't apply to them. Other people shouldn't have affairs, shouldn't take what belongs to them, shouldn't push the boundaries or even other people's triggers just to see what happens, shouldn't play in office politics, shouldn't gossip out of turn… but the rule book is sometimes not so clearly defined when it comes to their own behavior.

One of the biggest challenges of the EIGHT trigger to realize is that criticism without solution is simply criticism. Because the EIGHT energy is often harsh and brutal (but I was just being honest, he might say; she needed to hear the truth didn't she?), they can deliver 'truths' that no-one really wants to hear, in such a way that they can wound terribly. Honesty without compassion is simply cruelty.

The deepest dream of the EIGHT trigger? To control their world, and those in it. Control equals safety and predictability, you see.

'It's my stage, it's my play, you need to take my cue when playing your part', is a fundamental operating style of this energy. They don't like to be upstaged, and like the prima donna they are, do their best work when in the public eye. Take away their audience and the EIGHT crumbles and disintegrates, which has the potential to cause an identity crisis of gigantic proportions. This is the second saboteur quality of the EIGHT: 'To learn to see myself through my own eyes, and to LIKE what I see, not to constantly evaluate who and what I am, my successes or worth, based on the reflection I see in the eyes of the world'. In other words, EIGHTs need to become more self-referred, and less other-people referred.

NINE: Trigger and Sabotage Value

Our NINE Trigger is complex, multifaceted and often misunderstood, by themselves as much as by others around them. The NINE needs to learn to live in the real world, with real people and real situations, while all the while keeping their sense of make believe, of fantasy, of mystery and other worldliness.

NINEs can often feel as if they have a foot on two completely different planes. As we all know, the rules of engagement are very different in the real world compared to the rules that help us survive in the emotional world. NINEs are sometimes unsure of whether they fit into the real world, and what they have to do in order to be accepted there; likewise, the emotional world can be a fraught and frightening landscape when you don't have both feet planted on solid ground in the physical realm.

This is probably the biggest challenge for our NINE trigger: Stand strong, stand firm, stand in your own body.

NINEs have to find their emotional balance, their emotional core, and what they truly believe in life. For others it may be a suggestion that life would go better if they make friends with their emotional psyche but for our NINE it is an urgent undertaking that defines every aspect of their life.

NINEs need to realize that their right hand holds on tightly to the concept of the material world, physical safety and success, while their left hand is reaching out, grasping for emotional fulfillment, passion of purpose, and spiritual awareness. Unless the two hands work together, creating a link between these two very different worlds, the NINE will always feel as if he doesn't quite fit into the emotional and spiritual world, just as much as he doesn't really belong in the material world.

The minute the NINE gives in to ALL that he is, he becomes powerful beyond measure. If he combines the two facets of his psyche, the power of the manifest in conjunction with the promise of the non-manifest, he achieves and truly claims the title which we give to him: Old Soul, Wise Man, Shaman, bringing all the power of his ancestral knowledge into being.

The Sabotage Value is clear: Give in exclusively to the emotional world within and chaos awaits, self-absorption and selfishness reigns and everything degenerates into the cloudy wispy fog of fantasy and delusion. Surrender to the material and physical world, and non-fulfillment, demotivation, lack of purpose or reason destroys your power, insidiously gnawing like rats at your energy field, depleting your power and draining your belief in the world completely. There is an arrogance that comes into play when the NINE trigger devoids himself of his emotional power, just as there is a chaotic futility to the life of the NINE who swims exclusively in the ocean of emotion without any physical structure.

NINEs dream of a world that makes sense, where they can belong and fit into, where they feel safe and secure and flourish in. The minute they acknowledge to themselves that not only is it possible, but it is WITHIN their grasp right now, their dreams can come true overnight.

ELEVEN: Trigger and Sabotage Value

The ELEVEN energy as a trigger value is energized and intense, highly motivated and intense, over-the-top and intense, individual and intense, charismatic - and oh, by the way, have I mentioned intense?

The ELEVEN Trigger seems to have two speeds only: top speed, like the Duracell bunny running the marathon of his life and coming first, taking charge, flinging around orders and challenges like multi-colored M&M's - or stopped dead in his tracks, batteries completely worn out, unsure of the next step.

The ELEVEN looks around him, and wonders how come everyone else seems to have a life that goes according to plan: How come others seem to be content with the nine to five job, with the 2,2 kids, with the summer vacation in the same holiday spot every year? How do they even make that happen in the first place? Scratching his head in despair, he wonders if he was at the back of the line when the Gods were handing out the text books on what the life plan was supposed to look like, and how to put the plan into action.

When he is on top form, there is no-one more motivated, more captivating, more - well, more like a tidal wave really, sweeping you along at top speed on the surf ride of your life. When he is stopped dead in his tracks, he becomes more like a stagnant puddle of muddy water, complete with mosquitos and toxic sludge.

Sabotaged by his very nature of full throttle versus dead stop; of his motivation and charisma fighting his apathy; of his intensity and passion for more duelling with his desire to be happy with a quiet life, the ELEVEN has to find the balancing point between his own inner demons, and his own magical power. His deepest desire is to find this balance, but if he's honest with himself, he sometimes gets scared that he will get bored of a life with no dramatic ups and downs.

Of course, life is not meant to be a roller coaster. It may start off being exhilarating and exciting, but it has the capacity to degenerate into exhausting and draining at best, and disorientating and teeth jarring at its worst. When the ELEVEN is able to step back from himself, back from the situation, and into the witness and reflector mode, he will be able to see with the perspective that is required in order to bring the balance into being.

Paradigm

The paradigm is calculated by adding up the numbers in **the year of birth.** Like with all other numbers, we use the Fadic System of calculation and keep adding the digits up until we get to a single end number. If I wanted to look at the paradigm value of 2014 for instance, I would add:

$$2 + 0 + 1 + 4 = 7$$

If we go back to our example of the 3 September 1975, the paradigm is reflected by the year of birth which is 1975.

$$1 + 9 + 7 + 5 = 22$$

As we know, this is a Master Number, and so we do not need to dilute it any further.

However, I also like to use a second value when I am working with on the paradigm, which is the **century value**. This is reflected in the **first two digits** of the year of birth.

I believe that it sets the tone of how the paradigm value shapes itself, the mould that shapes out how the paradigm value is able to perform. So in our example of 1975:

Century Value = 1 + 9 = 10; 1 + 0 = 1. The century value is ONE

Paradigm Value = 1 + 9 + 7 + 5 = 22. The paradigm value is TWENTY-TWO

So we now have a **century value** of ONE and a **paradigm value** of TWENTY-TWO. The ONE provides a structure, a mould if you like, of how that TWENTY-TWO will behave.

What do we know about the ONE energy? It is male, focused, directed, individual, patriarchal, structured. This last century was certainly very male, very patriarchal, very focused and driven; a very different energy to this century with its prefix of TWO, which is a very feminine, nurturing number.

It makes sense that a TWENTY-TWO energy in a ONE **century mould** would tend to be more rigid, more restricted, more harnessed than that same TWENTY-TWO energy with a TWO **century value** would have. The TWO would give a far softer, gentler, perhaps more nurturing and self-tolerant framework for the TWENTY-TWO to relax into.

Think of the changes in societal thinking over the past 20 years or so. We have more women in positions of authority and power that ever before, in governments, politics, large corporates and start-up companies across the globe. There has been a groundswell of the softer (more feminine) skills changing the way we do business, as increasing numbers of people explore coaching, psychology, healing, intuition and spirituality in order to bring emotional intelligence into the business world. There is more focus on environmental issues, on humane farming, on health and nutrition, on sustainable agricultural.

Even spirituality, which for so long has been patriarchal as we have traditionally prayed to the male aspect of God (God the Father, O Lord our God) is changing as more and more people are beginning to honor Mother Earth, the Sacred Divine and the Goddess counterpart to the God energies.

WHAT EXACTLY IS A PARADIGM?

Essentially it means a system of beliefs or a certain way of thinking about something that has generally become accepted by society, the community, or by the family unit.

The paradigm value reflects the environmental belief system that we were born into AND the intrinsic belief system within which we were raised. We are products of our environment and the way we were raised UNTIL we start to question and explore and truly understand the meaning of the paradigm and the restrictions that it has placed on our interaction with the world.

This Paradigm Belief needs to be explored, understood and in some instances, challenged and overcome if it is hindering our progress through life instead of helping it. The Challenge is what we need to ask ourselves on a very deep, profound level: 'Although I may have accepted this belief for most of my life, do I really believe this to be true for me NOW? Do I want this to define my life and my interactions with the world around me?'

Remember that the mould of the paradigm, i.e.: whether it will be more overtly male or female, more ONE or TWO in its outlook and world view, is indicated by the **century value.** Essentially it means a system of beliefs or a certain way of thinking about something that has generally become accepted by society, the community, or by the family unit.

The paradigm value reflects the environmental belief system that we were born into AND the intrinsic belief system within which we were raised. We are products of our environment and the way we were raised UNTIL we start to question and explore and truly understand the meaning of the paradigm and the restrictions that it has placed on our interaction with the world.

This Paradigm Belief needs to be explored, understood and in some instances, challenged and overcome if it is hindering our progress through life instead of helping it. The Challenge is what we need to ask ourselves on a very deep, profound level: 'Although I may have accepted this belief for most of my life, do I really believe this to be true for me NOW? Do I want this to define my life and my interactions with the world around me?'

Remember that the mould of the paradigm, i.e.: whether it will be more overtly male or female, more ONE or TWO in its outlook and world view, is indicated by the **century value.**

Quick navigation links

If your Paradigm Value is a ONE, continue on page 120

If your Paradigm Value is a TWO, continue on page 120

If your Paradigm Value is a THREE, continue on page 121

If your Paradigm Value is a FOUR, continue on page 121

If your Paradigm Value is a FIVE, continue on page 122

If your Paradigm Value is a SIX, continue on page 123

If your Paradigm Value is a SEVEN, continue on page 123

If your Paradigm Value is an EIGHT, continue on page 124

If your Paradigm Value is a NINE, continue on page 124

If your Paradigm Value is a ELEVEN, continue on page 125

If your Paradigm Value is a TWENTY-TWO, continue on page 126

If your Paradigm Value is a THIRTY-THREE, continue on page 127

PARADIGM ONE

To lead, to achieve, to instruct, to tell others the how, when, why, where and what to do. To be individual, to stand self-reliant and independent of others. "I can do it myself, leave me alone, I want to do it my way".

Belief: THE ONE paradigm believes intrinsically that the only person he can fully trust is himself. "I can only rely on me. I know what I am doing. I only am able to be part of the team if I am leading it, if it's my team. My voice needs to be loudest and I need to make sure that I am heard".

Challenge: To listen and accept someone else's authority, to follow someone else's plan of action. To reflect with perspective and *then* decide on a course of action. To allow others to have a voice and express an opinion, even if it is different to mine. To give myself permission to trust that there may be a different way of doing things, but that doesn't mean that it is wrong. To accept that I don't always have to do everything for and by myself.

PARADIGM TWO

To support, to nurture, to keep the peace, to suppress individuality and personal opinion in order to avoid conflict. To be part of a team, to be part of a homogenous group within a larger family or social unit. To belong, to be wanted, to be included.

Belief: We need to hold onto a common identity and present a unified front to the outside world. If there are any weak parts to this family/ business/ group, we need to hold together and not allow the outside world to see how vulnerable or weak we may be. My weakness and vulnerability can be used against me, and I fear that. It is important that we hold firm to the common belief, the common goal and common purpose. It is only by swimming with everyone else that we can achieve our goals. The greater good is more important than the individual desire.

Challenge: Sometimes the 'greater good' can only be achieved by standing up and against the common belief, the wisdom or action of the day, not in supporting it. Sometimes partnership and union for the sake of togetherness is not what is best for you as an individual. Sometimes you need to allow yourself to sing solo. You don't always have to sacrifice and martyr your dreams, or suppress your desires for the family/business/organization.

PARADIGM THREE

To create, to manifest, to be part of the cause and effect, to experience joy and freedom. To act with responsibility and accountability for action and consequences.

Belief: I need to be free and unfettered so that I can breathe. I cannot create and manifest if everyone is breathing down my neck and watching my every move. Don't cramp my style by telling me what to do and when to do it.

Challenge: Being part of the cause and effect means becoming accountable for my role in it. Creativity and destruction is part of the same cycle, they are just different sides of the same coin. I need to accept accountability for my actions and accept that responsibility for the results of my actions rests with me. When I can harness accountability and consequence then I can achieve the full abundance that comes with unfettered manifestation.

PARADIGM FOUR

To find that point of balance, routine, rules, order and safety within the structure of society, relationships and work. To find the harmonious flow where things just work right; only then can I relax and enjoy life.

Belief: If I could just get all my apples shined up and balanced on the apple cart, then life will be good and safe and flowing. Once I have found out how to balance my apples, I believe I have found the Holy Grail of

Order, and so pedantically and rigidly, I will keep to that recipe to instill order. I need to be able to control my environment and people in my environment. Only by controlling the micro-issues can I feel safe within the macro-situations.

Challenge: Balance and harmony is not an end goal, a desired outcome only possible after hard work; it is present even within the chaos of life, minute by minute. The true challenge is to discover how to become balanced within yourself, so that you are not at the mercy of people, events and happenings within the world around you. In other words, you need to become self-referred and less other people-referred.

PARADIGM FIVE

To stand on earth, walk solidly with my feet on the ground, deeply connected to all aspects of life, knowing that within me I have the potential to touch the gates of heaven just as easily as I have the power to unlock the gates of hell.

Belief: I need to understand (and hopefully gain mastery) of my physical environment. Everything that happens in life is interpreted through the five senses. I can challenge, and cause people to act, through the sheer force of my personality. I want to win at all costs and so I see life a competition ground with ever changing rules.

Challenge: The choice to either be completely grounded, captivated by heavenly madness or seduced by dark desires is ultimately my choice. No-one can force me to choose a direction, I am the one who must embrace it in order to make it happen. I hold the power to influence, persuade and enthuse others; my challenge is to recognise the absoluteness of my own self worth without waiting for the world to give me permission to feel worthy. I do not have to win all the time. It is ok to allow others to be part of the process as well.

PARADIGM SIX

To nurture, to care, to feed and nourish, to bring order and balance behind the scenes. To create environments of caring structure and support where others can come and relax, and feel nurtured by the familiar, the comfort and the predictable routine of it all.

Belief: Any group works best in a defined structure, whether that is a family, a corporate, an army, or government. As long as we all know the common goal, and we all have defined areas, places and times of responsibility, and we all do what (and when, how, where and why) we are supposed to do, harmony and balance is assured.

Challenge: Retreating into safe and predictable routine just makes well-worn paths become deeply trodden ruts, marking deep grooves that define the borders of what is acceptable and what is not. Just because something has always been done a certain way, does not make it right. It just makes it predictable and known. The challenge is to step out of what is known and to re-examine whether it is still an appropriate belief or action, or whether there may be another way, a different angle, a new perspective.

PARADIGM SEVEN

Searching for truth, uncovering secrets, powered by a thirst to know it all. To discover the meaning of life and how it affects ME. To keep myself private and hidden from all except those that I trust and know that I can allow into the inner sanctum of my temple.

Belief: The truth is out there somewhere, and I will not rest until I find it. The truth is what I decide it to be, and I will insist that others accept my truth until I reach that point that truth is relative to the beholder.

Challenge: Admirable though the quest for truth is, the challenge for the SEVEN paradigm is not to descend into paranoia, suspicion, spying, mistrust and disbelief of others. It is hard work for others to constantly match up to your level of truth; recognize that different levels of truth exist, at different times, in different situations. Instead of demanding The Truth, try asking: 'What is true for this time, this place, this person, this situation?'

To know one-self is really the only truth that one can strive for. The truth after all is not 'out there'. It has always and only ever existed within ourselves.

PARADIGM EIGHT

To manage, to control, to direct, to govern, to judge. To understand the game of life and how to play it, in order to be safe, successful and satisfied on all levels.

Belief: I have strong ideas and opinions about how things should work, and I am not afraid to speak up and announce my thoughts or feelings to the world. I believe that I see the world as it is, and want people to listen to what it is that I have to say. There are rules and processes, and a right way to go through life and a wrong way. I can achieve anything that I set my mind to, and I can bring structure into chaos, because although I can understand the big picture, I really do get how important all the little details are.

Challenge: Others can respond to your 'knowingness' and opinions as rash, brash and a wee bit overbearing and arrogant. You may well know what is best for you, but you cannot prescribe what is best for others, unless they ask. The challenge of the EIGHT paradigm is to allow others to have their own beliefs and opinions, to live their life their way, - even if you do not agree with it – because that is their right. To be too opinionated and overbearing simply loses friends and isolates you, which ultimately disempowers you.

PARADIGM NINE

To flow, to dream, to conceive, to become a part of this world and this rhythm, to see things through to completion, to achieve closure and understanding of each stage of life before moving into the next stage.

Belief: I have never really been sure whether I fit in with the rest of the world. Often I feel as if I am standing off to the side, watching and observing, but not actually participating. I know that life is a flow, and sometimes I experience that flow as a melody that rises and falls and carries me with it. I watch others dancing to the song, but can't seem to quite hear the same beat that they do, can't seem to move my body or mind in the same way as they do. I want people to see that there are worlds within worlds within worlds, with a multitude of possibilities far more intriguing and stimulating to all the senses than the three-dimensional world they believe they live in.

Challenge: The NINE paradigm imbues its wearer with a certain mystical, fairy, fantasy, magical number. Whether they end up immersing themselves in fairy tales (or fantasy stories now that they are all grown up), or going after the pot of gold at the end of the rainbow, NINEs need to learn to keep their feet on the ground in the here and now, and that mysticism and magic is wonderful (and desired in fact) but chasing pots of gold at the end of the rainbow is a bit like building a castle in the air. It sounds great – and if you close your eyes tightly enough, you can even see it. But of course castles in the air are hard to live in. Your partners and family might get tired of watching you go off on another 'wild goose chase' leaving a trail of unfinished projects and false starts scattered in your wake behind you. The ultimate challenge for the NINE: start something, commit to it and FINISH IT. See it through to the very end.

PARADIGM ELEVEN

To understand, to challenge, to captivate, to inspire, to encourage, to illuminate. To find that central pivot upon which I can base the substance of my life; to realize what it is that lies at the core of me. As I find my center, everything comes into balance within me, like the central pivot of a see-saw. (Please also read Paradigm 2).

Belief: Life is a balancing act between extremes of passion and despair, joy and pain, love and apathy. I understand absolutely the realms of joy and happiness I am capable of, but am scared of my unerring ability to sabotage myself when things are going well. I can never seem to hold onto consistency in my life. Life is like a tide, it is constantly ebbing and flowing. I long for the moment of peace where the tide stops, the moment is now and that central peace becomes real to me.

Challenge: If ever there was challenge for the ELEVEN paradigm it would be to find consistency: in work, in love, in relationships, in finances, in personal aspirations. Often an ELEVEN paradigm will complain that they get the work and finances working perfectly, and the love life flies out the window. Or, they get the love life sorted, and then find that work ends up being dissatisfying; or they lose sight of themselves and their personal desires as a result. It comes from the ELEVEN habit of focusing with absolute intensity on one aspect of their life, almost to the exclusion of everything else. If I am in love that is all there is; if I am working on a project that captivates me, there is nothing else. This ability to focus so intensely is a double edged sword, as it brings fantastic successes… and even more fabulous failures. The lesson here? If you want to juggle loads of balls at the same time, that is absolutely fine; there is no-one more capable of multi-tasking than you. But DON'T for a single minute take your eyes off the balls until it is time to put them all down!

PARADIGM TWENTY-TWO

To create a bridge between differing perspectives, to connect possibilities and opportunities which support and encourage the development of something that is bigger than the sum of its parts. To be the link between the 'Castle in the Air' blue-sky thinking, and laying the corner foundation stone here on earth. To realize what it is that lies at the core of me: fairness, harmony, balance, nurturing, diplomacy, collaboration, and allowing that to be my ultimate expression in all endeavours and encounters. (Please also read Paradigm 4).

Belief: I am destined for something bigger than this, I can feel it. I am not supposed to be someone small, I am meant to be larger than life, I am meant to be a teacher, communicator, path-finder, guide for others to find their way. I struggle with the 'knowing of all this' and then the 'bringing it into being'. If I can sense it, why can't those around me? All I need is someone to give me the stage so that I can be as big as I know I can be.

Challenge: The challenge facing the TWENTY-TWO Paradigm is to recognise that yes, they *are* meant for something bigger than this. They *are* meant to be the bridge builder, the teacher, the guide, all of this is true. But teachers, guides, architects and builders need to a)learn their trade very well, so that they know their subject inside out and backwards. They need to b) practice what they do until they become the adept and well known for having this skill. They have to c) earn respect by performing consistently and with integrity, and then and *only then* do they earn the title of Path Finder, Guide, Master Teacher, Bridge Builder.

Serve your apprenticeship. Learn and hone your craft. Practice with diligence. In other words, the TWENTY TWO needs to earn his stripes before the world will listen. But once you have earned your stripes… ? Watch out world.

Your challenge is to be the Master of your Fate, not a jack-of-all-trades. As challenges go, they don't come bigger than that, do they?

PARADIGM THIRTY-THREE

We won't reach the THIRTY-THREE paradigm for a good couple of years yet. We won't be around to see it and, at that stage, I am sure there will be new understandings and new depths and secrets that will be revealed with time.

SECTION FOUR
Your Soul Purpose

LIFE PURPOSE OR DHARMA NUMBER

Your Life Purpose or Soul Purpose number determines the purpose, goal, and direction of your life. Put simply, we look at this number to reveal what drives your life's purpose.

It is a rare person who hasn't asked 'But what is it all about? What am I meant to be DOING with my life?' If I had a dollar for all the times I have been asked 'What is my life's purpose?' I would be a multi-millionaire by now!

Once our survival needs of having a roof over our heads, having enough food, being warm and clothed have been met, our attentions turn to WHO we have around us, who we share our life journey with. It is a human need to be accepted, acknowledged, included. We all have a deep drive to feel part of a group; acceptance equals safety, and therefore survival.

But once these needs have also been realized and we are to some extent assured that they will continue to be met as we move through life, we begin to ask ourselves far deeper questions. We start to search for that which will give our life meaning and therefore some level of understanding of what this human journey is supposed to be about. We strive to gain insight into who we are not just in relation to the people and elements that surround us, but also who we are in the in the context of the Universe and Cosmos that surrounds us all.

In other words, we want to find a PURPOSE for it all: For our reason for being *here*, in *this* body, at *this* moment in time. We long for something that tells us that we exist, that we matter. We long for some truth that validates who and what we are.

We hear of people who do great things with their lives, and imagine that Life Purpose means finding our 'own great thing to do' with our own life. It is something that we need to *do*, and the sooner we discover what it is, the quicker we can get out there and claim our greatness in the *doing* of it all. The paradox, of course, is this: the more we search for what it is we are *meant* to be doing, the more frustrated, disillusioned and despairing we become. We start the great novel, hoping that maybe we are destined to write, and will become the next JK Rowling; or sing on reality shows like "Britain's got Talent" hoping that someone else will realize our talent, and hey presto THEN our Life Purpose can START. Hey, it worked for Susan Boyle and Paul Potts, so surely that's how it will work for me?

Some of us spend our lives telling ourselves, "when this is over, then I can dedicate myself to finding my Soul Purpose." It's always "when the kids have left home" or "once I lose all this weight" or "when I finally have that qualification" or "when I get some money…"

If we are really honest, we would admit that there are times that we dream that our Purpose in Life is to do something really great and amazing, something that changes the course of mankind and history for ever - like come up with the wonder drug that cures cancer, or preach The Truth that enlightens everybody on the planet, or discover the lost world of Atlantis.

But what if our Life Purpose was not about DOING at all? What if our Life Purpose was wrapped up in *who are we now* versus *who we could be?* What if Life Purpose was all about BEING and there wasn't anything we needed to DO in order to fulfil it?

I believe that we come down to this earth with a set of skills, talents, dreams and abilities in place. If we can figure out what our skill-set is and how to use it, we can achieve anything that we set our mind to… and do anything that needs to be done.

I also believe we come to earth with a full set of insecurities, fears and self-made obstacles that stop us from being ALL that we could be, that prevent us from reaching our highest potential.

Our Soul Purpose, quite simply, is to overcome those obstacles so that we can harness the power of all that we are. Our Life Purpose is to step into our full energy, our full power, the full greatness of all that we are.

In other words, our purpose in this life is to LIVE with PURPOSE.

As we start to understand this value, which is calculated by adding your day and month of birth together, we start to understand what direction our Life Purpose can take us in… if we are brave enough to start the journey. This number reveals our inherent Destiny, what the Hindu's describe as Dharma. It is the very essence of why we are here.

Remember, this means that you are harnessing:

Quick navigation links

If your Soul Purpose is ONE, continue on page 131

If your Soul Purpose is TWO, continue on page 133

If your Soul Purpose is THREE, continue on page 134

If your Soul Purpose is FOUR, continue on page 136

If your Soul Purpose is FIVE, continue on page 137

If your Soul Purpose is SIX, continue on page 138

If your Soul Purpose is SEVEN, continue on page 140

If your Soul Purpose is EIGHT, continue on page 141

If your Soul Purpose is NINE, continue on page 143

If your Soul Purpose is ELEVEN, continue on page 145

If your Soul Purpose is TWENTY-TWO, continue on page 146

If your Soul Purpose is THIRTY-THREE, continue on page 148

SOUL PURPOSE: ONE

To stand in your own truth, your own beliefs, your own power.

The voice of the world is incredibly loud - and only getting louder still - as media of every description shouts out 'expert' opinions on what to believe and what is right. Celebrities have become preachers, talk-show hosts hold public confessionals, and politics have become state religions.

The Soul Purpose of the ONE is to draw back, stand back and reflect deep within on: 'What is my truth?'; 'What do I believe, deep within the core of me?'; 'How does it shape my actions, my thoughts, my behavior, my life?'

These are very deep questions, and the ONE will certainly recognize that many times during his life he has been forced to decide whether to ignore, deny, compromise or honor his own truth.

The ONE has to come face to face with the concept of what is true for him alone, irrespective of the truth it holds for those around him. He will have to decide what he really believes in, what he will stand up for, what truth he will live his life by.

When the ONE steps forward into his own truth circle, into his own belief system and owns it absolutely, no matter what the circumstance or who it is telling him what to believe or not. The moment he inhabits what is true for him and PUTS IT INTO ACTION, he truly stands proud within his Soul Purpose.

Standing in your own power means exactly that. It does not mean bullying or disempowering others in order to gain some pseudo-sense of feeling powerful. It is not about dismissing, negating or reducing another's energy in order to inhabit a place of power over them. It lies not in resisting or rebelling against another's power, or rules or regulations. Neither is it an energy that can be conferred by others or given as a status symbol demanding public authority and respect.

It is an individual journey, a private encounter with the self. A partner, a spouse, a friend, a boss cannot tell you what to believe, although they very well may try incredibly hard. In the same way we cannot, no matter how loud we may scream or shout the odds, force another to believe what is not true for them. We cannot take our beliefs from a celebrity, pop-psychology, or TV talk show, although the media and those around us will try all their powers of persuasion to make it so.

People with a ONE Soul Purpose will be forced to ask themselves, to deeply examine what they truly hold to be true. They may also have to accept that although it may be true for them, that it may not hold true for anyone else. This realization brings with it a challenge that asks us to have the courage, conviction and belief of this truth and to act on it so that others may recognize the power of our truth.

It's very easy to say that we need to act and talk from this level of truth, but the reality is that often, our soul truth or life truth is not consistent with the popular truth of the times or society in which we live. For this reason, people with a ONE energy as their Soul Purpose number may find that they have had to spend a lot of time on their own, or detached or apart (emotionally or actually physically) in order to come face to face with this concept called Soul or Life Truth.

SOUL PURPOSE : TWO

To support, to collaborate, to mediate, to serve.

'To serve?' I hear you mutter. 'How come everyone else gets a Soul Purpose of leading, or creating, or at least being the nurturer and healer, and I get stuck with a Soul Purpose of being a Servant?'

Serving is not to be confused with being a doormat! Sometimes when I say that the TWO represents the energy of the Servant, people conjure up images of Cinderella being left behind while her two ugly sisters flounce off to the ball. Cinders was left behind to clean up and scrub the floors, while her sisters got to put on the make-up and pretty dresses and dance the night away with Prince Charming.

The first part of this Soul Purpose is to recognize the true value of serving lies not in being submissive, manipulated and controlled to do others' wishes. Sometimes the TWO needs to learn to be quietly assertive, and not give in all the time simply in order to keep the peace.

Indeed, if you are honest with yourself, you will recognize the many times in your life where you have been a supporter of others' ambitions, projects or desires, sometimes to the detriment of your own. The challenge of the TWO Soul Purpose is not to sublimate your own desires because someone else's seems more important or more urgent… but to create mutually beneficial and symbiotic relationships where each gets fed and supported and held. You have the ability to create the most amazing networks around you by doing exactly this.

If the ONE energy is the masculine leader, the one who defines the direction (the one who rounds up the sheep and gets them all headed in the same direction in other words) then the TWO is the one who supports and encourages, who gently holds and compassionately waits for any stragglers, keeping the light burning so that the last ones home can see it burning in the darkness.

The TWO is the one who is able to pacify, heal rifts, compassionately supporting and quietly encouraging, bringing out the best in people and making them believe in themselves. They might not be the ones attempting to climb the mountain top, but it is because of their consistency of being 'there', of people knowing that they can be relied on to support from the sidelines, that others are able to achieve and become all that they dream of being.

We used to say, 'behind every great man is a great woman'. Modify that somewhat... behind every great achievement, there is someone who believed absolutely that the achievement was possible in the first place... and there you have the essence of the TWOs Soul Purpose.

Whether you apply this remarkable ability in a small manner in your own personal life or within your own family; whether you use it in the corporate and business world; whether you use it in a greater capacity of mediator and peace-making in politics or social structures, one thing is absolutely sure: When you inhabit this mantle as the supporter, the enabler, the empowerer of others to become all they are capable of becoming, you allow yourself to be everything you are capable of being.

What is that exactly? Non judgment, non-control, complete acceptance of who people are and the way they behave, non-manipulation of situations and people, supportive and empathetic and loving.

It is the most beautiful Soul Purpose.

SOUL PURPOSE : THREE

To create, to develop, to manifest into reality.

The true power of the THREE comes into being when it is able to harness the strength, individuality and truth of the ONE energy (the male energy of focus and direction and initiation) and combine it with the nurture and support and flowingness of the TWO energy (that female energy of gentleness and empowerment).

The child of these two magnificent opposing yet complementary forces is the energy of absolute manifestation, the joy of creation, the exuberant fusion of male and female to create a separate energetic form.

The THREE is destined to create and that may well be through art, painting, music, acting; through words, emotion, poetry, stories; through creating .beautiful living spaces or garden environments; or through the most divine cooking and baking. It is also just as likely to manifest in the board room, or in the research lab inventing a whole slew of new technical products. One thing is for certain - the THREE is drawn over and over to this need to bring something into being.

Our THREE needs to realize that he has all the raw materials existing within and, like the alchemists of old, has the power to transform mud into glittering mountains of gold.

Often the draw back to this absolute ability to manifest lies in a crippling level of insecurity and self-worth, and this holds the THREE back in a spiral of mediocrity instead of stepping boldly onto the pedestal of greatness. Most THREEs will be able to recognize the many times they have walked away from something that could have been amazing just that one minute too soon… or have gone against their gut to trust their most brilliant ideas with the wrong people, only to see things come crashing to the floor.

With a THREE as your Soul Purpose number, you will be no stranger to disappointment, projects or dreams that have just stopped dead, or dispersed into thin air suddenly.

Your purpose is to recognize the absolute power that sits inside of you, and that it needs no-one else to validate or clarify it, except yourself. Once you step into the power of your own Self Worth, you step up to be able to create, to manifest, to develop anything it is that you put your mind to.

SOUL PURPOSE : FOUR

To bring law and balance and harmony into being.

The energy of the FOUR is by its very nature supportive, stable, reliable and capable. It is the wooden support that the vine clings to as it grows toward the sun, supporting the weight of the grape cluster as it grows and matures. It is the table that brings solidness and function into the dining room, allowing us to place our plates on it, to sit at it while we eat and gain nourishment, to rest our elbows on in comfort and companionship after the meal has ended. It is the desk that allows us to place our work on while we are toiling away at our labors, or studying towards gaining more knowledge. Whether it is a solitary cup of coffee for one or a banquet for many, the table is the essential supporting element to function, abundance, comfort, and facilitate.

The FOURs Soul Purpose is to bring support and structure into being. Somebody once said to me that a FOUR was the most boring number of all, because it simply holds the frame work in place so that others can leverage off it to achieve greatness. I disagreed. The FOUR energy is the unsung hero of numerology, because it is the quintessential aspect in any endeavor. It is the keystone of any building from which the entire building takes its shape, design and function.

It is the umbilical cord to the space man while he is outside his satellite, keeping him connected with the ship, so he doesn't go hurtling off into space. It is the bungee rope that the adventurer gets tied to when she jumps off the bridge at Victoria Falls, to stop her from smashing head first into the Zambezi raging below.

It applies a force field to keep us on track and on the right path. Without the FOUR to keep us grounded, solid, stable, we'd all just go off on a random orbit, like crazy electrons in an over-excited hadron collider.

The Soul Purpose of the FOUR is simple, but that by no means reduces the purpose as simplistic or non-important. Her job is to bring balance, order, routine and structure into each and every aspect of life that she gets her hands on - and in so doing, introducing the concept of harmony into the lives of everyone around her.

Harmony when it is said and done is really quite simple. By following the rules of nature, support can flourish, and become a stable, consistent factor of our lives. It really is that simple.

SOUL PURPOSE : FIVE

To antagonize, to activate, to challenge.

We know that the FIVE in its power is physical, strong, present and because of this, it demands attention. You will find it impossible to ignore a FIVE. Whether they are in a brilliant, scintillating, dynamic mood, or a miserable, surly, depressive and argumentative mood they are just so THERE!

Love them or hate them, the FIVE demands to be seen, demands to be heard, demands to be validated, credible, noticed and, because of their unique command of their physical realm, notice them we certainly do.

The Soul Purpose of the FIVE is to step into ALL of this commanding ability, and to use it to challenge and stimulate, to force people to question, to examine - and ultimately take action. If the FIVE simply talks and does nothing, all they do is irritate the hell out of everyone around them and demotivate themselves into the bargain. FIVEs need to put their money where their mouth is and commit, step up and into, and be counted for what they believe in. Anything less will deplete them, drain them and leave an aggressive, arrogant, big mouth who, like the boy who cried wolf once too often, simply gets disregarded after a while.

While other energies might look at an appalling situation, like baby seals being clubbed to death, or the shocking conditions that livestock is raised and slaughtered in, and say 'gee, somebody should do something about it', the FIVE Soul Purpose is the one who steps up and shouts out 'what can I do to stop this or change that?' FIVEs seem to be have their little portable soapbox hidden in their pocket, and can whip it out at a moments notice to challenge others to **do** something, to stand up **for** something, to change the way things are done.

Because of this, the FIVE might find that at times they get excluded, or that others try to diminish their passion, zeal or determination. We ridicule what we cannot understand, we mock those whose passions don't quite echo ours, we try to control those who command the attention of others. It's human nature, but for the FIVE who throws their entire HEART AND SOUL into something they believe in, it can be very hurtful and cut them very deeply. Super-sensitive, sometimes chronically insecure, the FIVE Soul Purpose has to learn to recognise the worth and the power of his own efforts EVEN WHEN it seems that nobody else is taking a blind bit of notice.

What others say can have a profound impact on the FIVE because they don't respond well to criticism, and can sink into apathy and dejection saying 'what's the point of it all anyway?' The point is, change happens one person at a time. We cannot start a groundswell of movement to change situations on a global scale until we have had swelling of movement within. The point is that you need to live, breathe and act your truth, so that it speaks for you, consistently. The point is that unless somebody stands up and challenges the rest of us to change for the better, that we will continue blindly along a traditional status quo.

Change is not comfortable, sometimes it is downright scary. For some it feels like white water rafting down the Zambezi River while it's in full flood. Your Soul Purpose is to hold our hands and lead us toward that change in such a manner that we believe we can make the journey safely.

SOUL PURPOSE : SIX

To mature, to grow up, to take care of, to combine domestic harmony with corporate successes.

SIXs seem to make achieving their Soul Purpose look easy. They have this flair of appearing capable and efficient no matter what environment they are inhabiting at the time, whether that is the sorting out and taking charge on the battlefield in a war zone (or in a corporate office!) or taking the lead in a domestic or family situation. SIXs often have a calming, comforting, nurturing air around them that makes people relax when they walk through the door, safe in the knowledge that someone else will do the sorting out and taking care of. In an emergency, SIXs naturally know what to do and how to do it. They can rescue kitties out of trees or puppies out of burning buildings with equal levels of capability and calm. Certainly in a stressful situation they have the ability to soothe ruffled feathers and pour oil on troubled waters.

One SIX woman I know can rustle up a meal for the 5000 literally out of the 5 loaves and 2 fishes at a minutes notice. Another SIX I know was at the epicenter of the earthquake that hit Christ Church, New Zealand, at the beginning of 2012, and quickly got involved in setting up a first aid rescue center to help and assist others.

A SIX man I know runs a huge organization with the precision and clarity (and a little bit of an iron fist) but everyone knows exactly what needs to be done and when, which in turn brings security and comfort to his employees. And another man I know is the proverbial sergeant major in the army, setting the rules for his troops and ensuring that everything functions according to prescribed orders and regulations.

The SIX is superb at this, and his Soul Purpose comes out in its highest expression of service to others, to his family, his community. Just remember that while you are out easing the suffering of the world, you also need to bring some of this compassion, love and order back home with you.

Remember the story of the shoemaker's children? Their father was so busy courting the favors and approval of the community with the wonderful shoes he made, that he forgot about his own family's needs. While they were walking about in the middle of winter barefoot in the snow, he was sipping hot chocolate as he courted yet another important client.

The SIX Soul Purpose is also notorious for neglecting himself at the same time.

The purpose of the SIX is to keep his sights on nurture, and support, and harmony for everyone in his orbit, starting firstly with himself, then extending it to his family, and then – and only then – the larger community.

A healer is really only as good as he is healed, one can only give compassion when one truly knows the meaning of it for themselves, and nurture of the soul first and foremost is truly where it all begins.

SOUL PURPOSE : SEVEN

To find your own spiritual expression.

The Soul Purpose of the SEVEN is to achieve self-realization, however you define self-realization to be.

We are all searching for ourselves, searching in the mirror for the true reflection of who we are, but for the SEVEN Soul Purpose it is a driving force: To find that which makes sense of this journey called life.

The SEVEN can be so immensely focused, intensely connected on the matter at hand, which can lead at times to obsession, fixation and compulsion at its one extreme, or disinterest, disappointment and disillusionment at the other. The SEVEN wants to know, wants the answers, wants the real meaning of life – and like the hapless traveler in the Hitchhiker's Guide to the Galaxy, he cannot rest until he finds it out.

Anyone who has been around a SEVEN energy (wherever it appears in the number pattern) can attest to their intensity, focus and total absorption in the theme of the moment - whether that be positive or negative. They bring passion and intensity to whatever is occupying their brain and energy at the time.

What has to be remembered is this: Positive or Negative, constructive or destructive, empowering or completely disempowering, the SEVEN Soul Purpose will succeed at *whatever* they put their attention to. If they are being self-destructive, with negative self-talk, disempowering thoughts and limiting beliefs, they will succeed in breaking themselves down beyond their wildest dreams. If alternatively they put all their energy into empowerment, constructive activities and positive beliefs, that too will succeed beyond measure.

The SEVEN holds that choice in his hands. 'Whatever I focus on will grow' is something he needs to remember, and ensure that he puts his thoughts as far as possible on the positive, uplifting, empowering and constructive.

Self-worth, self-confidence, self-belief, self-knowledge, self-wisdom, self-empowerment, self-realization - to realize all of these are the Soul Purpose of the SEVEN.

And then, having discovered the key to it all in his own life, to facilitate the rest of us in getting there as well.

SOUL PURPOSE: EIGHT

To flow, to detach, to let it be.

The irony of course is that the EIGHT needs to be in control, hold authority in situations, be in command of the direction and focus required. The paradox for our so-in-control EIGHTs is that it is only in detachment, in allowing the flow and letting things find their own pace at times, that they will find the ultimate level of control of themselves, their life, their Soul Journey.

The EIGHT Soul Purpose will have to confront this issue of control in his or her life over and over again, before moving toward acceptance that really the only thing that we can truly control in this life is ourselves... and only then if we are truly honest with ourselves.

EIGHTs are generally superb at controlling situations, other people and themselves, so much so that they can manipulate others (ok, read that as *persuade* others if it makes you feel more comfortable!) without being aware that in the process they stand wide open to being manipulated and controlled by others in return.

With control comes judgment about what needs to be controlled; judgment about what is good or bad, what doesn't measure up, what is not quite good enough; judgment about whether someone else can do the job that has been delegated to them as well as it should be done, about what is appropriate or acceptable or agreeable.

In the world of the EIGHT, it all comes down to one thing: if it can be managed and controlled then it can be measured to a predetermined set of parameters. If it can be measured, then it is predictable. If it is predictable, then the world is safe.

By managing the macro-issues in the external world around them, EIGHTs excel in management, leadership, business, deadlines, orders and delegation. By managing the micro-issues tightly in the internal world within them, EIGHTs are often incredibly intolerant - of themselves above all else. Yes, they demand excellence and perfection, but are hyper-critical of themselves when they fail to achieve their own exacting standards.

The perfect metaphor for the EIGHT is the man who religiously, without fail, polishes the bars that surround him until they glisten and shine with the constant rubbing, without once realizing that he is polishing the bars of his own prison. As we pull back to see the picture in its full perspective, we see that the doors of the prison are standing wide open. He refuses to see the bigger picture however, and focuses only on controlling what is in front of him.

And therein lies the Soul Purpose of the EIGHT: To realize what is theirs to control, and what needs to be managed. To realize what is NOT theirs to control and so to stay out of it, or even to walk away from it, before it ends up manipulating and controlling them.

Two good questions for the EIGHT Soul Purpose to ask would be:

Does this issue have an impact on my life? If the answer is yes, then deal with it. If the answer is no, then the second question to ask is:

Is this any of my business? If the answer is yes, then again: Deal with it. If the answer is no? Let it go, it is none of my business.

SOUL PURPOSE: NINE

To combine 100% of the physical with 100% of the spiritual.

The purpose of the NINE is both the easiest and paradoxically the hardest Soul Purpose to realize. Easy because it demands just one action from us in order to allow that purpose to manifest, and hard, because this is the one thing that we humans struggle to do.

In a word, the Soul Purpose of the NINE is to Surrender.

That's it, that's all that needs to be done. Surrender to the concept that there is more to you than just the here and now, surrender to the inherent spirituality within and around you, surrender to the possibility that there is a Divine order to *all* life, and so therefore there is a Divine order to *your* life.

This is not to be confused with the human notion of giving up or giving in. Surrender brings the NINE to a place of unique personal power, over himself and his environment. Once he begins to accept that there is a certain unalienable flow to the Universe, to Life, to Relationships; once he accepts that he is part of that flow and so can neither dictate nor control it, he stops fighting the chaos of life and gives in to the order within the chaos. It is then that the NINE can reach a place where he can feel at peace and in harmony with himself and those around him.

More than any of the other number energies, the NINE stands in the doorway between the physical, tangible known world, and the unseen, unmanifest, unfathomed. Often though, the NINE will find himself turning away from one world completely to embrace the other… in other words, he either ignores the spiritual world in order to live his life 100% in the material physical, or denies the physical aspects of life in order to live 100 % in the spiritual.

For this reason, Ashrams, Monasteries, and Retreats are filled with people who hold a NINE Soul Purpose number, people who deny all aspects of the physical world (money, possessions, job, even relationships), in order to devote themselves 100 % to their spiritual world.

But the NINE Soul Purpose number is just as likely to deny their spiritual side completely in order to succeed in the material world of money, business, and property.

The full purpose of the NINE comes into being when he realizes that he stands in the doorway between the two worlds, and with full intent and conscious awareness puts one foot firmly in the spiritual world, and the other firmly in the material world, and creates a marriage of the two within him.

You see, the NINE was never meant to be a lone ranger, denying one aspect of himself in order to achieve another. He was meant to harness 100% of ALL that life has to offer; the mysteries and the material, the power and the potential, 100% of the physical and 100% of the spiritual.

MASTER NUMBERS

The Master Numbers are notoriously 'difficult' to master for one simple reason: the higher the Master Number, the longer it takes to 'master' its energy and vibration, and to understand the lessons and blessings that they bring.

The main reason for this is that, unlike the numbers 1-9, master numbers carry a combination of number energies with them.

- The ELEVEN carries the power of the ELEVEN, the ONE and the TWO.

- The TWENTY-TWO carries the full power of the TWENTY-TWO, but also carries the energy of the TWO, the FOUR and the ELEVEN.

- The THIRTY-THREE also, carries the power of the THIRTY-THREE, together with the THREE, the SIX and the ELEVEN.

Each number, as we have discovered, already carries its own authority and energy signature. To now combine all of those energy signatures into one master number can lead to confusion, turbulence, despair, apathy, elation, and ecstasy, all rolled into one. In short… it can be one helluva rough ride over the rapids until you discover how to manage your unique number combinations.

SOUL PURPOSE: ELEVEN

To inhabit the point of balance.

The ELEVEN Soul Purpose brings with it all the strength, direction and power of the ONE, the nurture, beauty and feminine psychological power of the TWO, coupled with all the charismatic polarized energy of the ELEVEN. It can be a tough juggling act to keep those three opposing numbers happy and harmonized, and so sometimes promises a bumpy ride for the one who holds an ELEVEN Soul Purpose number.

In fact until the ELEVEN Soul Purpose can find the point that balances them, they will always find themselves in a spiral of:

- Giving and doing and existing for everyone else;
- Being impossibly selfless, only then to get angry about being used or unheard or invalidated, under-appreciated and retreating into an orgy of selfishness;
- Feeling guilty about putting themselves first (I mean, really, how selfish can I be?) and ricocheting back into that endless cycle of giving, giving and giving some more until resentment takes over again.

It's a hard one to manage. They don't want to hurt other people. They really don't want to let others down, they truly want to be there for other people - but at the same time they want what they do and say to matter, to have an impact, to change and stimulate and provoke. In short, they want to feel as though their contribution to the world is valued and necessary – whether that be in a relationship, in business, or in saving the whales and the dolphins.

Yet they are often torn between helping others, which in ELEVEN-speak means more often than not denying themselves. They hover between giving and caring for others and the need to receive care and love for themselves, and therefore taken advantage of by those around them.

The ELEVEN Soul Purpose can then retreat into sarcasm, criticism, harsh words or into extreme withdrawal, all of which are a barrier to that feeling of being used and abused by others. This is followed by non-committal, non-action, non-participation while they lick their wounds.

Their Soul Purpose of the ELEVEN is simple. To find that point of balance between giving and taking, being used and abused, seen or invisible, accepted or feeling rejected. If you are an ELEVEN Soul Purpose, you will know that you have the potential to inhabit the extremes. Your way out is to find the balance: Get there, and life makes sense. Get there, and you can cope with **ANYTHING** that life throws at you. Get there and in reality you learn how to transcend the polarity and to truly live in that mystical heaven called balance.

SOUL PURPOSE: TWENTY TWO

To build bridges, to manifest, to bring practicality into fantasy.

The bridge builder of the TWENTY-TWO brings with it the stable, routine, builder energy of the FOUR, the feminine nurturing sometimes shy energy of the TWO, the polarized charisma of the ELEVEN, and the visionary blue-sky thinker that is the TWENTY-TWO.

Wow. Just dealing with one of these numbers is hard enough. Try dealing with all four all at the same time!

It's like trying to bath four little puppies all at the same time. Chaos, soapsuds, and water everywhere as first one puppy tries to run away then the other. Hold that image in your mind for a moment - controlling four wet wriggling slippery puppies all at the same time, and you just about have the idea of what it is like to have TWENTY-TWO as a Master Number.

Sure, you can be stable at times; sure you can be endearingly gentle and slow to warm up at times - but now marry those very complementary energies with the capricious charm and dynamic power of the ELEVEN in its full force - add in a large dollop of blue-sky thinking for good measure – and you have an absolutely unstoppable force of unbelievable potential!

The power of the TWENTY-TWO as a Soul Purpose number is to harness all of these energies: Stability and endurance, creation and grace, balance and extremes, vision and blue-sky thinking. The full capability of these combined energies adds up to someone we call the Master Builder, the person who can conceive of something so far removed from our reality, who can see all the possibilities and capabilities that exist, and then translate it into every-day language and bring it into reality.

I explained it to a client like this the other day: The TWENTY-TWO has the privilege of having his boardroom in the castle in the air. It is surrounded by blue-sky thinking, out-there possibilities, and rose-colored spectacled visions. But then he has the ability to walk out of that fantastical boardroom, down the castle steps, onto solid earth, and to transform his ideas into solid practical reality.

The Soul Purpose of the TWENTY-TWO is to simply do ALL of this. Think big, dream huge, imagine without borders… and then create the practical, real, and stable foundation for all that you imagine to manifest.

Of course, it all sounds so very easy. The risk for the TWENTY-TWO though is that he gets lost in the delights and wonders in the castle in the air, a little like Puck becoming enthralled and spellbound in a Midsummer Night's Dream, and losing all touch with reality. Or, on the flip side, he can become so grounded in reality and the 'here and now', that he never really gives himself permission to dream, and his feet never 'get off the ground'.

Again, like the ELEVEN Soul Purpose, TWENTY-TWO is a hard energy to manage, because of the many contradictions it brings with it. Dream but stay grounded. Imagine and build castles in the air, but don't forget to pay the mortgage here on earth with real dollar bills.

Like the ELEVEN, the trick is to find the balance and the synergy between the numbers. The TWENTY-TWO has to learn when is the right time to bring out the full power of the ELEVEN, or the stable influence of the

FOUR, or the endearing nurturing ability of the TWO, or the dreamer and visionary of the TWENTY-TWO.

This is a balance that unfortunately cannot be taught. It has to be felt, within, experienced and understood until it becomes an intuitive knowledge, and of course that only comes with the passage of time.

The old TWENTY-TWO truly becomes a master with each passing year, but he will be the first to tell you that it wasn't easy doing so.

SOUL PURPOSE: THIRTY THREE

To teach, to inspire, to save, to guide, to enlighten.

(This will only apply to only one birthdate in the entire yearly calendar: those born on the 22 November.)

We call this energy the Master Teacher. It has been likened to the Christ-energy, the one who searches for his enlightenment and, having found it, teaches it to others.

It combines the joyful spontaneity of the THREE in her full childlike glory, the healer, home maker, carer of others inherent in the SIX, the capricious charm of the ELEVEN dynamic because of her ability to inhabit the extremes of intense light and intense darkness, and then the full potential of enlightened energy within the THIRTY-THREE.

Four very intense energies which by themselves alone are hard enough to deal with. The THIRTY-THREE has to learn how to cope with all of these energies all at the same time. Not an easy journey by anyone's standards.

The THREE energy brings with it joy, exhilaration, unparelled enthusiasm and a massive 'come on let's get out there and try anything once' attitude. Life is for the moment, it needs to be lived and enjoyed and experienced is part of the THIRTY-THREE mantra. (Because of this factor, actually, many people with a THIRTY-THREE Soul Purpose energy both look and act much younger than they really are. I have two clients who are both THIRTY-THREE Soul Purpose, both of them are in their early 40's, and both look at least 10 years younger).

The SIX brings with it a need for safety and routine, nurture and caring – predominantly for those around us in our space, because the THIRTY-THREE doesn't like too much of senseless, traditional routine as they find it rather stifling and restrictive. This SIX energy makes way for exceptional nurturers and caregivers when it comes to others, (but not always so much when it comes to themselves). Sometimes, because they are so good at looking after the needs of others and taking care of others, they may find themselves surrounded by needy, emotionally weaker people, who feed off their strength and compassion.

The ELEVEN is polarized, dynamic, extreme, charismatic, dramatic and powerful in its ability to create or destroy, with a powerful force to be seen, needed, validated, wanted, to be of recognizable value.

And the THIRTY-THREE? This is the portal to wisdom, to self-knowledge, to enlightenment, to soul awareness, to cosmic truth.

The Soul Purpose of the THIRTY-THREE then is to find the key to unlock the portal, so that they can cross over and absorb the wisdom of All That Is… and to then step back over the threshold back into the world and make it available to the rest of the world.

But again, as with the other master numbers, the sheer contradictory pull of the numbers in this combination, make the finding of the key the equivalent of searching for the Holy Grail.

Some THIRTY-THREEs have sat in caves high in the mountains, hermitting themselves from the world in order to cross that portal. Some THIRTY-THREEs have given into the sheer abandonment and chaos of the ELEVEN and the THREE together (great at a party together this is true, because they can rile each other to greater and higher heights – or lower lows!). Some THIRTY-THREEs will choose the path of the SIX hoping that nurture and service will be the key that will unlock the portal.

Of course, as with all Master Numbers, it is only in the merging and blending of all of these numbers together than give the THIRTY-THREE that its absolute power. The power of this Soul Purpose is to harness ALL of its energies… the joy and exuberance and enjoyment of life in all its child-like glory; true compassion, nurture and caring for everyone and everything on the planet; the desire to change and challenge and stand up for something in life, and to encourage others to do the same; to bring balance into their own life and therefore into the lives of those around them; to sometimes stand apart from the world, in order to see what REALLY needs to be done in order to grow, to change, to become, to step up and forward into the next level.

The THIRTY-THREE as a Soul Purpose really is to take us all to a higher level of wisdom and being… but they first have to find out where it is and what it really means; spend time understanding and comprehending it all for themselves first and foremost… and then teaching it to the rest of us.

Not an easy purpose. No easy task at all.

This also means that the THIRTY-THREE Soul Purpose is likely to spend quite a large portion of their younger years alone. It is the hardest of all the energies to assimilate and understand, and so it keeps people who carry this energy walking a single solitary path for a while, as they learn to assimilate the full power of all that they are.

SECTION FIVE

Working with Universal Energy

What we have learnt up until now is what I call *Descriptive Numerhythms*. If we learn and understand the meanings of the numbers and the patterns in which they appear, we start to build up a very good DESCRIPTION of the person.

As we have seen in the previous sections, we start a "descriptive reading" by looking at the Life Path, then delve into the Skills and Talents, Triggers and Default Cravings, and Paradigm Values. We then examine the Soul Purpose and once we have these insights we start to build up a pretty good perspective of the person in question. We lay a foundation for an in-depth understanding of who the person is and how they are likely to respond in any given situation

All of this is, of course, exceptionally powerful information. We can use it to see apparent strengths and weaknesses. We can see what type of career or vocation the person is best suited to, whether he or she is likely to be successful in a particular endeavor or enterprise. We can look at the Descriptive Values to see how suitable a prospective employee candidate will fit into an existing work team.

We even can look at the Descriptive Values to reveal compatibilities and potential stresses between people, and use it to see whether a love match will work for the long term or whether it is only meant to be a passionate moment in time. When we look at the Descriptive Values we begin to understand why relationships and friendships succeed or fail.

(For more in-depth compatibility of love relationships, you can read our e-book: The Love Code, available soon through Amazon. This little book is devoted entirely to relationship compatibilities - what works and why, what doesn't and how to fix it, and what the relationship challenges and secrets are).

But there is another important aspect to Numerology, which I call *Predictive Numerhythms*.

If we understand even just the basics of how this aspect works, we can begin to predict what type of situations and events are coming up in someone's life journey, and give recommendations and suggestions of how he or she can best approach the situation and use it to their advantage.

PREDICTING FUTURE EVENTS

The Universal Year – both the current year and the coming (or even past) years are reflected in The Universal Year energy. By looking at this value we are able to see the prevailing energy that is in play at the time which *surrounds everything and everyone on the planet*. By examining this energy we can then see how it will affect global living conditions, as well as that of the country we live in. We also have an indication of the global stress factors that are likely to be encountered and the challenges facing the society in which we live.

The Personal Year – when we look at this value, we can see the current year indicators, as well as the coming year's cycle, as it *personally* relates to the individual. We look here to see how the global energy of the Universal Year is likely to impact on the person, as well as specific personal issues and stresses he or she is most likely to encounter.

The Personal Cycle – what each day, month and year has to offer as we move forward into the future, in terms of strengthening, challenging or weakening my Life Purpose or Life Path.

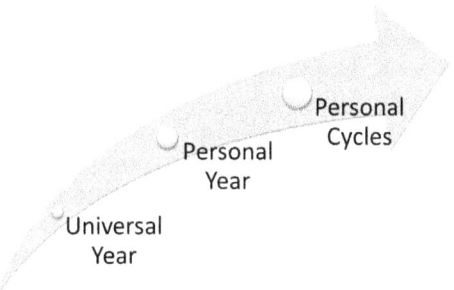

THE UNIVERSAL YEAR

We have already learned that Numerology works with the energies of 1 – 9 (with the Master Numbers of 11, 22 and 33 included into the mix), so it won't surprise you to learn that we also calculate the cycles of years, months and days in cycles of 9.

In the previous chapters, we explored the Paradigm Value that is inherent within the **year of our birth**. This value conveys the global belief and the global energy that surrounds us as we are born, and how it shaped our beliefs, our challenges and our value system.

It is exactly the same with the **current year** that we are living in… it holds an energy that shapes the global belief and the global energy system of everyone on the planet.

Have you ever wondered why it is that the entire planet seems to go through cycles of global financial crisis, or periods where violence, war and revolutions start breaking out in hot spots across the world? Numerology offers up an explanation: There is an energy that is called the Universal Year, and it surrounds the world with a blanket of energy into which *everything* comes into contact - not just humans, but *all* living creatures. It also has a tremendous impact on *anything* that has a cycle of energy or dynamic movement to it, for example, the stock exchange, governments, weather, armies, societies.

Everything is influenced by the Universal Year energy: the planet, her tensions and stresses, as well as the environment and its influencers.

At the time of writing, it is currently 2013. As we have done many times since we started this journey together, we begin by taking the YEAR and using the Fadic System, we reduce this to a single digit:

$$2 + 0 + 1 + 3 = 6$$

The Universal Year for 2013 is therefore a 6. If we follow that same system, 2014 will be a 7 Year, 2015 will be a 8 year. 2016 becomes a 9 year.

2017 = 1 year; 2018 = 11 year; 2019 = 3 year, and so on, and so on.

As we move through the different Universal cycles, each numerical energy brings its own specific pressure, release, or challenge to the earth, which may encourage the expression of a certain aspect or suppress another.

Up until now we have used the numbers to describe a value or character trait within a personality. Can it really translate into describing the energy of the year as well? The answer, of course, is yes. We can adapt and use the number descriptive values very readily to describe not just a person, but a place, a time, or even an event.

As we discovered in the last section, the year energy has a powerful influence over us. It carries with it the energy, the belief, the paradigm of the time… the 'pool of consciousness' that I spoke about in the beginning of the book that surrounds us all. It has a powerful impact on everyone and everything, as it surrounds all of us on planet earth; we are constantly breathing it in and out all the time, saturating our physical bodies with every breath that we take. You can imagine that as we breathe this energy into physical bodies, that we are absorbing it all equally into our mental, emotional and spiritual bodies at the same time.

Most of you working with this book will have been born in the previous century (wow, now *that's* a BIG phrase!). In other words, in 19 something or other. As we now know, we add the 1 + 9 to reach a 10, and then further add the 1 + 0 to get to our end digit of 1. And as we also know, the ONE energy describes the male energy.

This means the **century value** that describes the consciousness, the belief and paradigm that we were raised in was very male, quite patriarchal, with more focus and reward on action and accomplishment than on communications and empathy. Recognition and acceptance was dependent on who you were, what you did, how much you earned, what status and therefore authority you carried within the community. Religion was patriarchal and male dominated, priests and ministers were ALWAYS male (indeed it has only been over the last twenty years that we have seen the emergence and acceptance of women in the clergy), and the female side of things was an euphemism for weak and fragile and needing to be taken care of (and told what to do).

Women in the corporate world seemed to shrug off their feminine qualities as they walked through the doorway and felt as though they needed to emulate male behavior in order to succeed and get ahead.

But times are changing, rapidly and one of the biggest indicators for this is that we are now in a **century value of TWO** which emphasizes the feminine aspects (as opposed to just a few short years ago, when the dominant paradigm value was male). As we move deeper into the 21st century, we are seeing values and beliefs being challenged and changing before our eyes!

In religion, more women are achieving acceptance and recognition in their leadership roles within the traditional clergy. In alternative religions there is a powerful resurgence of the Sacred Feminine Divine as more people become aware that the Feminine Goddess energy is the duality counterpart of the Male God energy. All over the planet people are re-awakening to the knowledge that life is supported in a myriad of interconnections as they once again honor and protect Mother Earth.

In the work place we are seeing the emphasis turning from control and dominance to collaboration and communication, as the power of the TWO begins to influence career choices and corporate direction. Increasingly, people are turning to Emotional Intelligence and Cognitive Techniques to increase productivity and improve team dynamics.

More women inhabit positions of authority throughout the corporate and political arena than ever before, in developed countries across the globe. Indeed, developing countries have powerful women voices, and in traditional male patriarchal societies such as the Middle East, women are speaking out and are finally being heard.

Self-sustaining communities are beginning to spring up all over the place, as increasing numbers of communities turn to trading and bartering as a legitimate form of payment for services and products.

Political structures of old, dictatorial regimes in countries all over the world have toppled as the people have joined together (collaboration) and screamed their need for a more representative governmental rule in their countries.

So much change in such a short time… and still the changes are happening, causing us all to adapt, to evolve, to grow as this TWO energy challenges and provokes us into new ways of being and living.

This **century value** impacts on the **Universal Year** quite dramatically; we are in 2013, which is a SIX year, but it is a very different SIX energy in a **TWO century value** than it would in be a **ONE century value.**

These two dynamics influence how the year will shape up. Think of it as the diving board from which the diver spring-boards to get into the pool. The pool is the SIX energy – the **Universal Year Energy**. The diving board is the **century value** (how he enters into the pool) and this is the TWO energy.

By now we are very comfortable with the meaning of the numbers, and so we can almost intuitively predict what the energy for the specific cycle will be. Here is a very brief description of the global meaning of the Universal Years, from 1 – 9:

ONE Universal Year

An important year for new developments in industry, technology, society. It brings new ways of thinking about things, exploring new possibilities. Many will feel the surge of creative desire as the planet responds to an outpouring of renewal, strength and power. What is set in motion in this year creates the foundation for the rest of this NINE year cycle.

TWO Universal Year

TWO cycles bring a quieter energy that is good for reflecting, collecting, planning, assisting others, seeing both sides, working together, collaborating. In short, supporting what was started in the ONE year. The focus is on relationships; not just personal and intimate relationships, but also those at work, with the community, with society. On a global level, it impacts on governmental, political and business relationships as well.

THREE Universal Year

A THREE cycle is a cycle of creativity, communication and getting causes, projects or creative endeavors noticed. It is a year demanding social awareness and interaction, of becoming aware that which each of us do in our own little lives has a ripple effect on our environment and those around us. Vice-versa, it also asks that we behave with responsibility and awareness to ourselves and others. The danger of a THREE year is that it pulls us off course, chasing after sparkling, interesting tangents that have the potential to simply be pleasant diversions at best, or to lead us round in circles, achieving very little. It asks us to be aware and accountable for our actions.

FOUR Universal Year

FOUR cycles are the time for practical, step-by-step productivity, for observing the rules, and for creating solid structure. After the wild creativity of a THREE year, the FOUR year brings purpose, balance and structure so that the creativity can continue to flourish. It is a year for putting down roots, and building from the ground up. This is a year of hard work and personal discipline, and can bring obstacles and limitations and imbalance as much as it can bring balance and harmony.

FIVE Universal Year

During the FIVE cycle, we get a break from routine and find ourselves experiencing new people, places and perspectives. This is a year of change and action, (sometimes rebellion and activism!) of moving forward, of challenging old habits and traditions to see if they still are appropriate. It shouts at us to "get out of the rut" in terms of the way we think and act. A year for massive global social involvement and change, for humanitarian awareness, for environmental projects, for thinking of the bigger picture.

SIX Universal Year

SIX cycles bring us back to family matters and remembering our commitments and responsibilities within our family, communities and societies. What are our Values? What are our Morals? This year will bring these into sharp focus. Investments, property, developments, homes, home financing all are highlighted in the SIX cycle, as is Health, Nutrition, Food for the nation. It can be a year of either collaboration and support, or sergeant major type rules, regulations and routine… or both aspects can fight it out in some crazy combination! It can also be a year of personal growth and maturing, and a year of stress and chaos. Sometimes our greatest growth as a species is done after our biggest trials.

SEVEN Universal Year

SEVEN cycles are interesting cycles for the global energy. Often this year comes hand in hand with frustrations and obstacles in tow, highlighting obstacles and uncertainties on a world-wide scale. It is often called a Year of Destiny, because it asks us to reflect deeply on who we are, what we believe in, what our truth is, what collective truths about the society we live in that we have come to believe or disregard, what is it that holds real meaning, real value. It is a year where what is hidden or kept secret can become known, where secrets and lies become exposed for the untruth they really are, where the Media and Community Leaders will be held accountable for what it is they ask us to believe.

As we pull our attention inward and we examine our life, our purpose and our truths, it can inspire us to achieve our full potential in any situation.

EIGHT Universal Year

A global focus on money and the making, lending, borrowing, use of money. Power and the use and abuse of power comes into the spotlight, as it relates to political, corporate, governmental power… all the way down to the power that we spurn or appropriate in our own lives. In a good strong EIGHT cycle, this represents the culmination of all the work and discipline, creativity and knowledge of the previous seven years for the good of all on the planet; in a negative EIGHT year, it is all about power-mongering and money management which allows the rich to keep on getting richer and the poor to continue suffering.

The EIGHT cycle challenges us to put our money literally where our mouth is, and take action.

NINE Universal Year

A year for completing the cycle. I have always thought of a NINE year as the end of one phase, and the beginning of another. Much like a pregnancy that has to die so the baby can be born, the NINE year asks us to wrap up and finish what needs to be completed with honor, so that we can start anew with new projects and focus areas in the new up-coming NINE year cycle.

This means that on a global energy communities and countries will be presented with the fruits of their labors over the past years; they will be asked to commit to finishing them. The alternative of *not finishing* means that we enter the beginning of the next NINE year cycle from an energy of non-completion and non-commitment, rather than one of fulfilment and success. Often a difficult year of challenge and assessment, we need to take care not to make excuses for non-performance and non-completion, or worse, blame it on someone else, all of which is highly possible in the energy this year brings.

In essence, we are asked to let go of what doesn't work, in awareness and accountability so that we can clear the way for the new cycle. It brings change, uncomfortable change in some instances, but necessary on a global scale. It is only from this perspective that we are able to start to dream again of new possibilities and growth potentials.

Personal Year Cycles

The **Personal Year** indicates how the global energy interacts specifically on an Individual Year. 2013 has brought some very interesting challenges and stresses to my family, but each one of us has responded to our changing circumstances differently. This is because the energy of the year *interacts with our own personal vibration*, which in turn sets up its own dynamic bringing specific behaviors and actions to light.

Working with this energy reveals very specifically what needs to be accomplished, suppressed, avoided or focused on during the course of the year.

To calculate your **Personal Year,** we take **the Life Purpose Number** and add to it the **Universal Year Value**. Remember, the Life Purpose Number is the sum of your **day of birth** plus your **month of birth**.

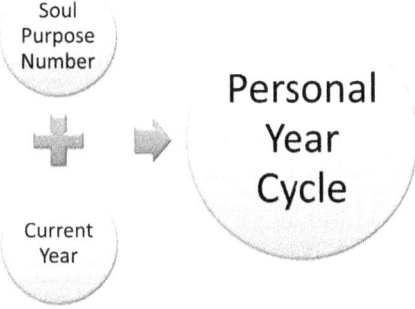

In our example of 3 September 1975, the day = 3 and the month = 9; this gives us a value of 12, which we further reduce by adding the 1 + 2 = 3.

We take this 3, and add it to the Universal Year number, which for 2013 is a 6 (2+0+1+3).

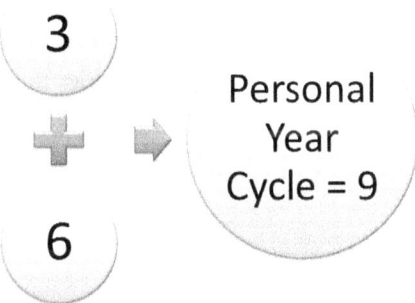

The personal year would be 9.

ONE Personal Year

A ONE year is the beginning of the new NINE-year cycle and brings with it a glorious energy of NEW beginnings, complete with fresh starts, original ideas, interesting impressions, new opportunities and increasingly strong personal beliefs. Because it is inherently a male energy, it is focused on action, accomplishment, direction and focus. This is a year for fresh directions, for breaking free of old habits and debilitating beliefs, and for allowing yourself to start a new project, career, business or life cycle. It asks that you be open to direction, and ready to act when the time comes with decisiveness and individuality. It is not a time for dithering and delaying. Be ready with your plans and hopes as early into this year as possible, so that you can move forward with clarity and purpose.

Remember, that what we put in motion this year will stay with us for the rest of the NINE year cycle, so this is a time to pay serious attention to the foundations you are putting in place.

At the end of the day, you are the only one who can decide what is best for you. Get all the information you need to make the right, informed decision, and then GO FOR IT. There has never been a better time than now to take control of your own life direction.

Challenges: You can expect to be challenged on what you believe, and what you are prepared to do and say as you put these beliefs into action in your own life. If you do not act or do not decide, don't be surprised when things are decided for you. The words of that old poem, 'I am the master of my ship, I am the captain of my fate…' are the perfect description of a ONE year, if you allow it to be so.

TWO Personal Year

A TWO year is that beautiful female energy of nurture, empathy, collaboration and integration, and it really is the perfect supportive energy to follow the action-oriented and decisive focus of the previous year. This softer energy allows us to nurture those ideas and directions that we have (hopefully) already implemented in the previous year, to integrate them into all aspects of our lives, so that they can grow and develop and mature.

This is a year for relationships, for resolving (not walking away from) conflicts, for nurturing the meaning and depth of intimate partnerships and for encouraging the growth of business, community and friendship networks. This is a year where it is *who* you know and *how* you deal with them becomes far more important than *what* you know. Think of this year as cogs turning within the machine of focus and achievement. Each cog is important, no cog has a greater or lesser role. If only one cog ceases to turn, then the entire machine grinds to a halt. This year, **you** are the essential cog in all aspects of life that surround you. Whatever you do, however you turn, impacts on not just those closest to you, but everyone around you.

Challenges: This is a year that focuses on relationships – with yourself most importantly, but also with the core relationships around you – in your intimate relationships, with friends and family, with colleagues and associates. What is your relationship style? Is it supportive and nurturing, or critical and judgmental? We often find in a TWO year that our relationship communication style gets mirrored back at us in the fulfilment of the promise: What you put out there, comes back to you.

THREE Personal Year

THREE Energy combines the power and direction of the Male ONE, with the softness, nurture and collaborative skills of the Female TWO, to create their incredibly accomplished child, the THREE. If we follow this metaphor to describe the energy, the ONE year would be the ideal time to release a new project or start a new business venture – the birth of the baby, for a metaphorical allegory. The TWO year is when we nurture it, guide it, allow it to grow in a safe space, watching its every move to make sure that is it safe and secure – teaching the baby to crawl and to become secure in its new environment. The THREE year is when we have a toddler running around, full of energy and vibrancy, learning, discovering, laughing, enjoying – falling down, making mistakes, hurting themselves, feeling unsure or insecure… but then getting back up again and starting all over again to run around as they explore, discover, and exhilarate in the sheer joy of being.

(** Of course the image of the baby is simply a metaphor for whatever it is you are wanting to create!)

It can be a beautifully social year with lots of new friends, interesting situations, exciting encounters. Get creative… get *wildly* creative this year! Speak, act, draw, create, garden, bake, sing, make music, make babies. If you can't do any of these things, then surround yourself with people who can. Allow your own creative talent to express itself as you give your dreams free reign: what are your greatest ambitions? dreams? talents? Dream Big. Dream Wild. But please, make sure that you allow yourself to DREAM.

Challenge: This is a year that asks us to invite passion and vibrancy into our lives. It asks us to think bigger, wider, further than ever before. Like the toddler whose steps are still uncertain, who falls down as he is learning to walk, we can expect to stumble every now and then. But, like the toddler, we HAVE to get up again, we HAVE to keep running. We cannot give in to insecurity or uncertainty, because that kills the THREE energy. Passion and vibrancy bring with them an energy of creativity and lateral thinking, of bringing brand new concepts into focus. The more we allow ourselves to really explore our environment, the more accomplished we become… and the more ready we are to see what comes next! Toddlers rarely go unnoticed. Their enthusiasm is contagious. Exhausting sometimes, but contagious. If you want something that you are doing or involved with to be noticed, the THREE year is the perfect time to harness all your energy to make this happen! This is a powerful, intense, glorious year if you allow it to be, or one of non-accountability, non-responsibility and insecurity. The choice, as always, is yours to make.

FOUR Personal Year

A year of deciding what makes you stable and then allowing yourself to put down roots which can establish you in strength and safety. Roots are vitally important in that they hold us firm and solid so that we are able to get out there and do what needs to be done. After the glorious abandon and vibrant passion of the THREE year, it is time to become more solid and dependable, to allow the projects that you are working on to mature and consolidate. It's time to act responsibly, reliably and consistently, not just for you, but also for the people who rely on you.

It is a year that asks us to put routines in place, to establish some law and order in our affairs, to create balance, harmony and consistency in all aspects of our daily lives.

Challenge: After a year of running around and getting noticed, it can be hard to calm down and concentrate on deliverables… like meeting deadlines, cementing all those relationships that you enjoyed creating in your THREE year, focusing on the bread-and-butter aspects of living, like money, rent, grocery bills, insurances, pension funds, etc. This is often a year of knuckling down to some serious hard work and accountability, which for some people can require an enormous amount of dedication, discipline or sheer will power. A FOUR year gives us the ability to have all of our apples balanced on the apple cart, as we achieve balance and conformity and consistency in our lives… or conversely, to be a year of complete and utter chaos as balance flies out the window, and all our apples land bruised and battered in the mud. In the words of the tortoise who raced against the hare, 'slow and steady wins this race'.

FIVE Personal Year

A year of action, communication, challenge, provocation and activism. A year of enthusiasm, physical power and energy. A year of extremes.

In your FOUR year you have had to learn how to dot the i's and cross the t's as you strived to create and maintain balance in your life. In a FIVE year, we want to shout out to the world how we are doing. It is a year to stand up and be visible, to announce our intention and assume our place on the pedestal of public recognition. It is a dramatic year that demands that the people around us validate that we exist, that we matter, and that what we do in life matters. A great year to advertise and promote yourself and tell the world what you personally have to offer!

A FIVE year asks us to take more risks than normal, to go the extra mile. 'Travel!' it screams at us. See the world! Or maybe, try a new sport, join an amateur dramatic society or expand your thinking by volunteering at some charity or social organization. This is a year to make new friends and meet new people. Don't be afraid to own your opinion and to voice it.

Challenge: The FIVE year heralds CHANGE in capital letters. Some people find that they change relationships (or the dynamics of the relationship change). Some people change jobs and careers, or their homes. Some change countries; some change who they are, and the way they think. In some FIVE years, we change the people we have filled our lives with as some relationships come to a natural end. Some change for the better, by taking charge of their life and their environment; some for the worse, by throwing it all to the dogs. The challenge is this: Be the Change that you want to see around you. It starts with you. It starts this year. (Oh and yes, great year to pay attention to your health and nutrition and to stop smoking once and for all!)

SIX Personal Year

A year which forces us to focus on our family and the responsibilities, obligations and interactions we have within our familial groups. It is a year which signifies family, home and investment, so it also hones in on any investments we may have, any property issues regarding house or land, and the long term financial planning that we need to do to take of our future safety.

The SIX energy often indicates caring for others, being aware of the needs and energy levels of those around us so that we can support, encourage and care for them, with compassion and non-judgment. Like the FOUR year, it is a year of hard work, of discipline and routine, of commitment and consolidation. SIX years are very important for personal growth and maturing.

Challenge: A SIX year demands that we become aware of the roles that we play at different times within our family structure, and the responsibility and obligations that accompany each role. I may be a wife and mother with my own family, and this of course demands a certain level of commitment and obligation – to my husband, to my children. But I am also a daughter, with a mom who is getting older as the years go by. I am a daughter-in-law, with an extended family commitment and interaction. I am a sister. Each role demands that I play it with awareness, honesty and respect for myself and the other person within the relationship, something that is not always easy in this age of broken families and shattered relationships.

It asks that we occupy each role with compassion and nurture and caring – for the other person, but also for ourselves. SIX years also place a large focus on the home, the land, and the family investment, and so it is a year where you need to pay attention to those long term investments and pension funds for your old age. This is the year to fix the house and make your home your space of refuge and calm in the world. This is also the year to fix the family relationship to what it is that YOU need, with honor and respect and compassion for all.

SEVEN Personal Year

The SEVEN energy offers a period of introspection, of self-analysis and awareness. This really is an internal reckoning of our lives of *what we have* versus *what we want*, in conjunction with *what we are prepared to do to get it*. In some ways it offers us an opportunity to withdraw from the chaos and demands of the world in order to reflect on what is really important in life. Our internal belief system (not the one we say we believe in, but the truth of who we are) starts to grip us and forces us to ask the question: Is there more to life than this?

The SEVEN year holds the potential for great spiritual awakenings and growth, for awareness of deeper psychological and metaphysical meanings to this journey we call life.

Challenge: For some people, a SEVEN year is monumentally uncomfortable, challenging us to explore the layers of our truth and to announce what is true for us. It can feel abrasive, harsh, stressful, and actually that is exactly what it is meant to be. We don't search for the meaning of life, or what our Soul Purpose is, when things are going well. It is only in the darkness that we search for the light, and so often people who are going through a SEVEN year may feel alienated, pressurized, depressed, directionless or isolated, as they find themselves stripped of old beliefs, thoughts and ideas that no longer hold any truth for them.

EIGHT Personal Year

I call the EIGHT Year a Platform Year, because this is a period in time that demands that we get our stage straight and level so that it can be the platform that we can build anything on. We want our structures – whether that be a marriage or a business project, a community development or an investment scheme - to be long lasting, to have impact, to carry weight, to be powerful, to stand firm, and this is essentially what an EIGHT year allows us to do.

It carries the emphasis on control of our life AND our environment in order to create true sustainability. It is the energy of the corporate, of finance, of wealth, of judgment and discernment of what will work (and what won't).

Challenge: EIGHT energy is meant to be discerning, to add perspective and clarity, all of which too often turns into Judgment and Criticism as the EIGHT tries to control not just his life, but the lives of those around him. Management is not control; it is about recognizing the skills and talents of those around you and drawing them out so that they can be used to their fullest potential. The EIGHT year is renowned for bringing struggles and obstacles as we try to get everything completed on time and to come in on budget.

Money is a key focus here for the EIGHT year: how to earn it, sustain or improve on your concept of abundance.

NINE Personal Year

A year of endings, of completion. A year of assessing what works (and therefore keeping it) versus what no longer works (and needs to be released and let go). NINE signifies the energy of completion, in both Numerology and the Tarot. It is a natural ending, the small death so that rebirth can begin anew and the cycle can begin all over again.

I have always thought that the analogy of pregnancy fits this NINE energy perfectly. It takes nine months for a baby to grow inside the womb. In order for the baby to be born, to take on its new identity and claim its own energy, the pregnancy needs to come to an end, to die as it were. As the pregnancy ends, the baby begins a new journey, but it can only do so because of the ending of one state so a new one can begin.

This death, this ending is necessary, essential. In fact, if the baby is not born in time, the placenta begins to calcify and deteriorate, meaning that the baby no longer is able to get the nutrients it needs to sustain life inside the womb. Left too long inside the womb the baby – and mother – would die.

The NINE year asks us to examine what we need to let go of, what needs to come to an end, in order that the new cycle of life can begin.

Challenge: Endings are not always neatly packaged like the last page of a novel, or a beautiful sun-set scene on the movie screen. Some endings are kind, gentle, and inevitable, but some are bloody, cruel, scarring us for years afterwards. It may be a belief system, or a self-limiting action; it may be a relationship that belittles you or a job that demeans you; it may be a political, religious, or personal belief; it may be none of these things, but simply an awareness that I am ready to *be* someone new, to *do* things differently, to *let go* of what no longer serves me, in order that I can walk through a door of different perspective in this next cycle coming.

The challenge of the NINE year however is not just facing the ending; the challenge is recognizing that UNLESS we let it go, we run the risk of bringing it with us into our next NINE year cycle and repeating it all over again.

Not easy, but necessary. Repetition brings reduced options and limits our perception of possibilities ahead. Completion opens the door to new horizons and new potentials.

Remember

It is important that you do not read the **Personal Year** in isolation. Everyone has a 9 year cycle, everyone experiences that same movement of energy… however, it is vital that we remember we will not all REACT to that energy the same way.

Think for a moment of the classic THREE energy, who often has conflicting needs for being looked after and fighting for freedom. When he finds someone or a structure that will look after him and make him feel safe, he is apt to fight against it in a knee jerk reaction to claim his freedom. How will he react in a FOUR year, which demands that he examine structure and act with forethought and responsibility? How will he accept accountability and consequence?

Right. He probably will find it remarkably stifling and suffocating, and find himself getting incredibly stressed as he feels the walls closing in on him. But put a FOUR energy in that same space, and she is far more likely to relax, to calm down, to feel safe within the predictability and routine of it all.

If we are reading a FIVE energy, and see that they have a FIVE year coming up, we might want to head for cover. Our FIVEs are by nature physical, and they are just as likely to be the destructive tornado as they are the grey pool of slush after a long hard winter. How they react within a year that says "throw caution to the winds, take risks, unleash your inner adventurer" is anyone's guess! If they are unpredictable already, you don't have to think very hard to imagine that placing them in a year of unpredictability might be the very best – or the very worst – thing for them.

But for a TWO energy, who by his very nature often plays things safe? Or a

SIX energy, who puts everyone else's needs before their own? If we place them in the middle of a FIVE year, we may be very surprised at the effect of this "move, grow, expand, become" energy on their outlook in life.

Always remember that the energy of the year always, always interacts through the filter of our own personal energy field.

Personal Month and Day

It stands to reason that if we can calculate our Personal Year Cycle, that we can also calculate our own Numerhythm cycle within the year, in days and months. Why is this useful?

Personal Month: This allows us to see our own cycle of energy during the year. It helps us to calculate when is a good time to start a new project or a new venture; when our personal energy is more conducive to focusing on relationships or family issues than on business and financial issues; how to prepare and plan for times when our energy may lag or slump, or when there is a potential that we might get side-tracked on a tangent of distraction.

If you have ever gone through slumps of disappointment or depression, or found yourself in a cycle of negativity and procrastination, it can sometimes feel as though it is going on for ever with no end in sight. Working out our Personal Numerhythm can give us back a sense of WHAT we need to do, and WHEN is the best time to do it, in order to feel that we are in control of our lives.

We calculate the Personal Month Cycle by adding

It stands to reason that if we can calculate our Personal Year Cycle, that we can also calculate our own Numerhythm cycle within the year, in days and months. Why is this useful?

Personal Month: This allows us to see our own cycle of energy during the year. It helps us to calculate when is a good time to start a new project or a new venture; when our personal energy is more conducive to focusing on relationships or family issues than on business and financial issues; how to prepare and plan for times when our energy may lag or slump, or when there is a potential that we might get side-tracked on a tangent of distraction.

If you have ever gone through slumps of disappointment or depression, or found yourself in a cycle of negativity and procrastination, it can sometimes feel as though it is going on for ever with no end in sight. Working out our Personal Numerhythm can give us back a sense of WHAT we need to do, and WHEN is the best time to do it, in order to feel that we are in control of our lives.

We calculate the Personal Month Cycle by adding

Day of Birth + Month of Birth + Current Month + Current Year = Personal Month

So, if I was born on the 3rd September, and the current month is October 2013, the calculation would look like this:

$1 + 9 = 10$, $1 + 0 = 1$. My Current Month is ONE.

So, if I was born on the 3rd September, and the current month is October 2013, the calculation would look like this:

3 + 9 + 1 + 0 + 2 + 0 + 1 + 3 = 19

1 + 9 = 10, 1 + 0 = 1. My Current Month is ONE.

PERSONAL DAY

Just as we go through a Personal Year and a Personal Month cycle, we also go through a Personal Day Cycle. This gives us more immediate feedback about the kind of energy surrounding us during that specific day, and we can plan our action steps on a 24-hour cycle as opposed to a monthly cycle.

This is calculated by adding:

So if today was the 2 October 2013, we would calculate it like this:

3 + 9 + 2 + 1 + 0 + 2 + 0 + 1 + 3 = 21

As always, we would reduce the 21 to a 2 + 1 = 3.

How would you treat the different energies of the Personal Days? Again, you would need to translate it through the filter of your own Personal Soul Purpose Number (the sum of your day and your month of birth) to see how YOU are likely to react to a specific energy.

The following descriptions of the Personal Day energies might give you some clues as how to best harness the energies of the specific day.

ONE Days

1. Sometimes we need the courage and the strength to walk through the door that is standing open in front of us. Today asks you to recognize that there are opportunities in the here and now, just waiting for you to step into.

2. Today remember: Assertive, not aggressive. Compassionate not

critical. Supportive, not sarcastic. To yourself most importantly!

3. A good day to concentrate on empire building. Who do you want in your empire, what territory do you wish to claim, and how do you want to rule it?

4. Your management skills are hotter than hot today, whether you are managing a corporate office, an unruly bunch of teenagers on tour, or a kindergarten. As you lead, others will surely follow.

5. Is it on the plan? If it is part of the plan then do it. If not, ask yourself whether this is just a diversion, a distraction, a red herring? Is this going to be a massive waste of time and energy? Be clear on what the REAL benefits will be at the end of the day. If there are none then don't even go there.

TWO Days

1. A wonderful day for intimate moments with your partner. I know, I know, intimacy is supposed to be spontaneous, but in this day and age where life is so busy, we just don't have time for intimacy unless we consciously plan for it. Today, send some sexy sms's to your special someone, have a naughty phone call, and make a plan (once the kids are in bed and the dishes have been done) to do some deep eye gazing and gentle kissing and hand holding. Good for the soul, good for the heart, GREAT as a stress reliever, and trust me, you'll sleep like a baby afterwards!

2. A fantastic day for team work, for joint collaboration, for group activities. If you are part of the team, ask yourself how can you facilitate this group to maximize their enjoyment of the project and of each other?

3. Sometimes we need to put our shoulder to the wheel, put our head down and work hard, ignoring everything and everyone else around us. Sometimes though, our best work is done by meeting, talking, connecting and networking. There is strength in networking

today. Leverage *who* you know, and who *they* know. You may be pleasantly surprised with the results!

4. Give those people in your support team a big thank you today. Recognize, validate, acknowledge and verbally honor the contribution they make to your life and what it means to you. Whether it is your partner doing the washing up after supper, or your secretary bringing you a cup of coffee after a hard day; whether it is your mom taking the kids off your hands for a few hours, or your best friend helping you with your homework, today is one of those days to say 'I appreciate what you do for me.'

THREE Days

1. A day to give it ALL you've got. Whatever you have on your plate, give it your full attention and your full energy. Put your foot flat on the accelerator, and full steam ahead. Don't hold yourself back, not one single iota!

2. Put on some loud pumping music and dance. Pick up the baby in your arms and dance. Do the vacuuming to the disco beat and take the ironing to a whole new extreme level. Nothing gets the endorphins pumping quite as brilliantly as some really loud music! Of course if you are in the office, you can't quite turn the volume up – what will Ms. Jones in Accounting say to that? – but you can put a spring in your step, run up and down the stairs instead of taking the elevator, and use your office chair as the magic roundabout, whizzing around and around and… until you make everyone as dizzy as you are! In short, make today a full-on day.

3. Today, get creative. If you sing or play music, let it flow. If you write, haul out your trusty little note-book and start writing. If you paint, draw or take photographs, allow your visual eye to record the beauty you want to capture. You might think you don't have a creative bone in your body, but quite simply that is not true. Explore with color, experience with your senses, experiment with

words… and allow your mind to run wild, releasing your imagination completely.

4. Today is the perfect day to develop that ad campaign or web site, to work on the book, to conjure up magic with your magic wand. It is a day where you can leap over barriers, no matter how high they might be, a day when you can reach up to the moon and capture a few stars while you are at it. A great day for any activity that expands your life.

FOUR Days

1. A perfect day to check the fine print on the sales documents, read through those legal contracts, prepare the tax return(!) or to get to grips with that tutorial for next week's lecture at university. Today is all about detail; paying attention to small stuff, reading through the lines and understanding what facts and figures are really being presented.

2. Think twice before you take your wallet out, and buy that new lounge suite/ pair of shoes/ Harley Davidson/ summer holiday in the Caribbean. Do you need it? Can you afford it? Is it what you need, want, desire? More importantly, will you still want it a year from now when you are still paying it off on your credit card? Take a deep breath, tell the sales assistant you would like to think about it a little longer, and go for a walk in the fresh air (or at least a strong espresso!) before you make up your mind. If it makes financial sense as well as emotional sense then go for it. But if your heart is blackmailing your head, rather sleep on it for a few days before committing yourself completely.

3. I know, I know, it's a horrible job, but some days are better suited to it than others. Sorry to say, but today is a good day for cleaning out the cupboard under the sink, the filing cabinet, or the sock cupboard. Donate anything you haven't used or worn in the past two years. Throw out holey socks, chuck out any empty jars and

bottles that have crept back into hiding under the sink, or Tupperware lids that no longer fit any of the sandwich boxes (I swear those things multiply by themselves!) Go through the CD collection and make sure the right CD's are in the right case, but be sure to put your favorite song on the player while you are doing it. I know it's not a nice job, but it needs to be done!

4. Today, take a piece of paper and make three columns on it. In the first column, list those things that are do-able for you to do today, taking care to list no more than 6 projects or activities. In the second column, list those things you want to achieve in the coming week. In the last column, list those things you want to pay attention to by the end of the month. Make sure that your items are do-able and achievable within the time span you have allocated for it. And then when you get to the end of the day, and you cross off the last thing on your list, give yourself a small reward for staying focused, centered and clear, and actually FINISHING IT ALL. Over the next week and in the coming month, cross more items off your list. Sometimes, we need to see our priorities written down in black and white to stop ourselves from dithering on a million and one other things that add no real benefit to the our lives. Today, put your focus on those few things that really do need to get done. Never been a better day for it!

FIVE Days

1. A good day for stepping out of your comfort zone, and for challenging yourself to reach higher, be bigger, take on more responsibilities, achieve more. Superman was just a quiet little journalist until he dared to put on his cape and underpants and soar out into the skies. Dig deep and find the Superman inside you. And, just as a reminder, buy a pair of Superman pants on the way home!

2. Today remember, that there is a bully in every sandbox. When we

were kids, it was just sand that got thrown in our faces. In the corporate sandbox that many of us have to play in, the bullies out there will use every trick in the book to get ahead at someone else's expense - only instead of throwing sand, it´s often reputations, integrity and performance that gets flung aside. Two things to remember: firstly, like the sandbox it really is all just a game, so don't take it personally at all. Don't give the situation or the bully any more of your attention or your power than it has already taken from you. And you are old enough now to decide whether you really want to play with bullies like this. If you don't, get out the sandbox, dust yourself down and calmly state: 'I don't want to play like this anymore.' Bullies can only exist when they can exert fear or control over us. Take that away and what do you have? A fat little kid with no friends.

3. A day for window shopping, for cruising car show rooms, for spending time imagining the island you are going to buy when you finally write your best seller. Make a vision board and put up pictures of the dream house, that trip around the world, the year off from the pressures of life in a country village in Tuscany. Dream it so BIG that you can almost reach out and touch it, you can smell it. Feel the saliva pooling in your mouth at the thought of fresh Italian bread straight from the oven, with cheeses, plump olives and bright red tomatoes. Yes. Just like that.

4. How are the vitamins and minerals going? Do you take healthy supplements or do you just supplement with a big Mac every now and then? Sometimes our need for additional vitamins and minerals is greater, depending on what is happening in our lives. For instance, a great deal of prolonged stress can deplete Vitamin B in our bodies, a long hard winter with minimal exposure to sunshine can rob our bones of vital Vitamin D. The older we get, the more our bones leech Calcium and Magnesium. Why not schedule a hair analysis and see what vits and mins your body is needing right now, so that you get your body in the best condition it

can be in?

SIX Days

1. If you have a garden, today is a good day for gardening and getting your hands dirty. If you don't have a garden, settle for either re-potting some plants, or maybe creating a balcony plant box. At the very least, go for a walk in the park and breathe in the fresh energy of the outdoors. Good for the soul.

2. A really good day to present your ideas on how to grow the department to your boss. A great day to look at expansion plans for the business. A fantastic day to try to get all your colleagues on the same page, hunting after the same goal. Today, you are in a good space to encourage team work and collaboration.

3. Thinking of buying or selling property? This is a fantastic day for property investment, whether you are making that all important purchase of your first house, or downscaling the family home to buy something smaller. Good day to maximize property for financial benefit.

4. Thinking of furthering your studies, or expanding your knowledge with a new course or workshop? Today brings heightened awareness of academic pursuits and studied knowledge. It doesn't have to be signing up for a formal 4 year degree with the university; perhaps it is a weekend workshop, or a training session presented by your company. Either way, it is expanding for the mind AND career, and that can only be to your benefit.

SEVEN Days

1. Thought for the day: Make today about the team. There are days to shine your own star, and days to ensure your efforts support the greater goal of the collective energy. Try to be inclusive,

collaborative and empowering of others on SEVEN days.

2. Today is about communication with integrity. Remember, in all your dealings and interactions with people around you, that we all see and hear things differently relative to our own individual perspective of reality. If in doubt, say: 'Can I just check with you. What I *think* you said was… is that correct?' Misunderstandings happen all the time, but today we need to be extra vigilant that a little misunderstanding doesn't snowball into a destructive avalanche.

3. Today is one of those key days when, if you allow it, you can easily enter the zone. That zone where perfection, expertise, knowledge and wisdom reside… yes, that zone. Some people get there by exercising until the brain releases enough endorphins. Some people get there by narrowing their focus exclusively to the matter at hand. Some people get there by meditating and tuning out the rest of the world to go deep within. It doesn't matter which technique you use. All you need to know is that, within your reach today, there is a massive pool of excellence, just waiting for you to dive into it.

4. A day for absolute sheer bloody hard work. Head down, shoulder to the grindstone, focus until the job is done. Try to minimize distractions so that you can keep your attention on what needs to be done. There will be time a'plenty to relax when the field has been tilled and the seed has been planted, but until then, use the sunlit hours and get it done.

5. Take the day off from technology. Completely. From sun rise to sun down, spend a day being human again. And try to schedule a technology free day into your diary every couple of weeks. Too much technology really does fry the brain. Really.

EIGHT Days

1. Thought for the day: Perceive and be aware, but don't judge.

Comment and clarify, but don't criticize. Stay in control of yourself, but don't direct and control others unless they ask for it.

2. A brilliant day for organizing, leading, managing, directing, telling, and just plain taking over and being the boss. There are days when we need to follow the direction of others... but that is definitely not your job today. Rather, it is time for you to inspire, lead, tell, motivate, empower and instruct. Take charge, and see how much you get done!

3. Budgets, business plans, bossy boots. It's time someone (you in other words!) takes charge and gets things moving, otherwise this ship will never leave the harbor, the tide will have turned and it will all be too late. Use your considerable talents to get things moving! And soon!

4. If people think you are preaching at them and get mad at you for telling them what to do today, just give them space. You are prone to being a wee bit bossy today, and could appear a wee bit strong minded. Not a problem generally, but you may find some people are super sensitive right now about told what to do. Instead of taking it as advising guidelines, they might read it as criticism and sarcasm. They'll get over it sooner or later, but in the meantime, keep your head down and only give advice and guidance if they ask for it.

NINE Days

1. Thought for the day: Be the river. Just let it flow, let everything that happens today to just flow. Don't get hung up on it, too attached to it, worry too much about it, or build a stressful or anxious relationship to it. Be the river, and just let it flow, and then, let it go.

2. Sometime during the day find time to schedule a 20 minute meditation time. Go within and feel the body, and consciously relax. Go without and feel the energy field around you and allow

it to become at peace. Expand your mind, heart and senses and feel yourself as a part of this great big Universal energy of life.

3. Sometimes we find that we have to let go of people and relationships in our life that have served their purpose. Sometimes it is a belief system, a habit, or a behavior that needs to come to a conscious end. Today be aware of that in your life which no longer serves you, and with respect and honor for the role it has played in your life, let it go.

4. An ending of cycle day today. What needs to be wrapped up, completed, finished off, signed off, or just plain let go of? Finish it today, so you can start fresh tomorrow, with fresh energy and ideas for the situation at hand.

ELEVEN Days

1. Aim for as much balance as you can today, because this is one of those days where the energies are at absolute polar opposites. You may feel absolute love and joy in one encounter, only to plunge headlong into paranoia and suspicion in the next. As you move through the day be aware if you are feeling overwhelmed by feelings of anger (like road rage) or despair, depression and anxiety, or complete gratitude and thankfulness. It is one of those topsy-turvy extreme kind of days where everything is exaggerated and blown out of proportion. If you can, get into bed and pull the covers over your head until tomorrow but if like the rest of us you have to face the day, keep coming back to your own point of internal balance - no matter what the day throws at you.

2. Get out there and give the performance of your life. This is a brilliant day for unbelievable attention and recognition from your peers – so don't try to be a shrinking violet, don't get stuck in the wings, don't be modest and shy and demure. When the spotlight starts shining your way, HOG IT, and then give your best

performance ever.

3. Ever wanted to write your own book? Host a TV show or be on the radio? Ever wanted to act in play, or direct documentaries? Do you tell yourself off for dreaming crazy dreams and then go back to your normal routine life? Leave celebrity lives for the celebrities, right? Why? EL James was just another housewife before she wrote '50 Shades of Grey'. Oprah was just a journalist who persevered, worked hard and believed until she became the icon she is today. Why are those people any different to us? Answer: they're not. If you have always held that dream inside of you, today, right now, this minute… do something to start it and get the ball rolling.

4. Sparkle, scintillate, tease, captivate, mesmerize, inspire and above all, Have A Bloody Good Time. Today is about the external aspect of you, about how others see you, respond to you, interact with you. As you ACT extroverted and passionate, you have the power to sweep them away on the surf ride of their lives. Just remember to deposit them safely on the beach afterwards!

SECTION SIX

Putting it all Together

So much information to absorb isn't there?

It seems overwhelming at first, but as I said in the beginning: the more you work with the numbers the more of an energy signature they take on in your own mind. After a while, you begin to feel the rhythm and the flow that each number vibrates to, the way it resonates within you when you think about it… and the numbers then start to take on a life of their own.

The trick is to keep working with them until you become familiar with their shape, taste, feel and dance.

Case Study

All the way through this book I have used the date: 3 September 1975 to illustrate how to calculate your Numerhythms. At this point, I would like to show you how it all comes together so that you can understand the flow of it all, using Rosalie's date of birth as our Case Study.

Step One: The Life Path

We always start off our journey into Numerhythms by calculating the Life Path, which as we know by now is calculated:

Day of Birth + Month of Birth + Year of Birth = Life Path

We write this as:

$$3 + 9 + 1 + 9 + 7 + 5 = 34$$

Which we further reduce to a single digit:

$$3 + 4 = 7$$

What do we know about the SEVEN energy? We know that people with this energy often over-analyze things and think things through in great depth. They have the potential for great clarity and can focus in on an issue to the exclusion of all else. They have high standards, and are very intolerant of themselves and others when they don't reach them, sometimes appearing critical or argumentative to others. They can hit the "zone" where nothing else exists for them but what they see in front of them… whether that be work, pleasure, family, achievement, or a problem that needs to be solved. We know that SEVENs can see-saw between emotions, sometimes making it hard for others to understand them. They can be loners, wondering where they belong, or if they fit in a group or community of people. Often looking for meaning or purpose to life, and a reason to understand what it is all about. SEVENs are rarely able to let sleeping dogs lie!

At this point, I turn to this diagram, and start writing out those points that stand out the most for me:

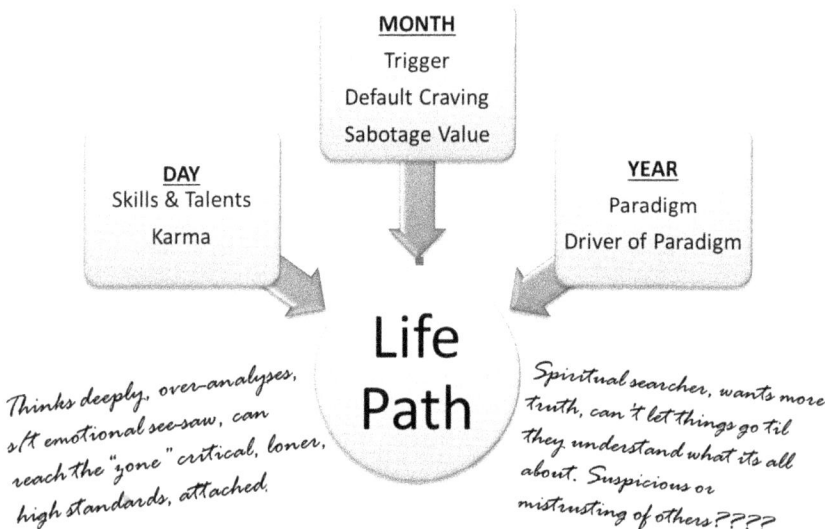

What Rosalie has to say

Rosalie says this is quite descriptive of her. If she has a bad experience for instance, she replays it over and over again in her head, in a "he-said, she-said" mental loop for ages until she is able to let it go. She recognizes that she can get very attached to issues, which is not always emotionally healthy for her. She also can be quite suspicious of others' intentions and motives, not in a paranoid way she says, but more in a way of "show me that I can trust you before I go and give it all to you". She has often felt that she doesn't quite fit in, and has felt lonely at key times in her life even though she has been surrounded by loads of people. And yes, she has always searched for understanding and to be understood since as long as she can remember, would actually say that it is one of the driving forces in her life.

Step Two: Fleshing the LIFE PATH out

Talents, Skills and Karma

Rosalie was born on the 3rd September, so her Skills and Talents Number is THREE. We are now able to start fleshing out what we know about her, by adding these qualities into the mix: childlike, imaginative, capacity for wonder and magic, sometimes emotionally childlike, insecure at times, sometimes uncertain what to do with responsibility or accountability. Sometimes, she probably wonders how she got herself into "this mess, this time round?" Lateral thinking, quite creative in how she goes through life, with the ability to make things happen, but probably lacks stickability, letting things just drop without finishing them. Good at castles in the air, but needs practical help in building foundations. Thrives on a reason to do things.

Trigger, Sabotage Value and Dreams

Rosalie was born in the 9th month (September) and her Trigger and Sabotage Value is a NINE. This is also the number of her inner-most craving, her secret dreams and desires.

This tells us that Rosalie is both conflicted by the depth of her emotional capacity and her longing for material safety and security. At times, she will shun one for the other exclusively, and other times will vacillate between the two. In desperate moments, she may feel that she doesn't fit into either space, which can raise insecurity and self doubt until she learns to be her own rudder. She has the capacity to be the bridge between the two extremes but she needs to own all that she is first. (Interesting, she shows this ability also in her Life Path value. Whenever you see a double pattern repeating like this it tells you to sit up and take notice: the effect will be magnified and manifest very strongly in the person's behavioural patterns).

Fearful and inspired by her emotional vacillation versus material need, she needs to understand her own journey and her own core before she can harness those creative and magical skills and talents of the THREE, and also before she can "grow up and into her own sense of self". At times she will reflect back to the world *what she thinks it wants her to be*, as opposed to who really is.

One of the things that Rosalie will have to come to terms with in her journey is her concept of Death and Loss. This doesn't mean she will lose everyone she loves, far from it. What it does mean however, is that through a myriad of little deaths, little losses and endings, she will discover who she is… but because loss is often a painful process, she will fear it and resist it before she is able to embrace the truth that loss brings. Sometimes we have to strip away all the obstacles before we see who we really are.

Paradigm

Rosalie's birth year is 1975, which we calculate as follows:

$$1 + 9 + 7 + 5 = 22$$

Her century value is 1 + 9 = 1 which tells us she was born into quite a male orientated, goal and achievement focussed, status centred society. It is patriarchal, meaning that concepts such as religion, government, finances, corporates, etc, were all based on an energy of masculine ethics, value and qualities.

Her paradigm value is 22. Quite an expansive, creative thinker, sees opportunity and possibilities, can be a blue-sky thinker. Struggles at times to make things concrete but when she does they have the power to really work. Can be an inspired teacher. Sensitive, feminine, soft, sometimes hurt by what others say or do… or conversely by what they DO not say and do. Likes to build bridges and networks, able to see power in relationships. Wants to do something to help or improve the lives of others, can sometimes see the world through rose-coloured glasses, and is truly surprised when others don't see the world the same way.

Our diagram is beginning to take on more detail and we can now start to see that repeating patterns are emerging, namely:

- Rosalie will struggle with self worth and inner doubt, and will often sacrifice her creativity and imagination, her inner emotions and desire to understand things at a deeper level. She has a need to fit in with the world and this demands that she "grows up and becomes responsible".

- She is not just sensitive: she can be super-sensitive.

- Rosalie has a need to be accepted and validated for who and what she is. What people think of her is sometimes more important than what she thinks of herself.

- She has a very deep spiritual need to understand life at its deepest levels and this drives her to analyse and sometimes over-analyse her situation and environment.

- She has two conflicting patterns going on: one where she trusts too easily, and another where she is suspicious of others' motives. This tells us that she needs to learn to listen to her own inner voice in making decisions, as she will be manipulated and pulled by what other people want from her.

- Creative and very lateral minded but often sacrifices that creative ability in order to try to fit in with the real world.

- Walks a narrow path between the emotional and the material world. Based on her sensitive nature, she could be highly intuitive; because she is very highly intolerant and critical of herself (and sometimes of others) she could just as easily struggle with emotional challenges such as depression or anxiety.

- Loss is a profound way of stripping obstacles from her, and she will have found herself challenged by loss and endings in various ways during her journey.

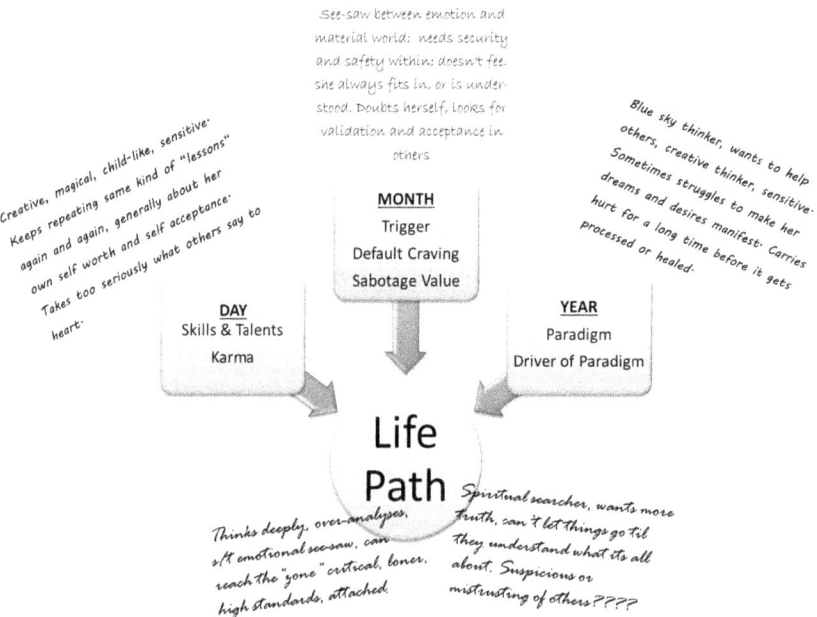

STEP THREE: THE SOUL PURPOSE

As we know, we add the value of the Day of Birth to the Month of Birth to calculate the Soul Purpose. Rosalie was born on the 3 September, which gives us a 3 + 9 = 12. 1 + 2 = 3. Her Soul Purpose number is a THREE, and as we know, the Soul Purpose of the THREE is simply: **To create, to develop, to manifest into reality.**

"The THREE is destined to create, and that may well be through art, painting, music, acting; through words, emotion, poetry, stories; through creating beautiful living spaces or garden environments, or the most divine cooking and baking. It is just as likely to manifest in the board room, or in the research lab inventing a whole slew of new technical products."

Rosalie has a double THREE going in her numbers: A THREE as her SKILLS and TALENTS number, and also again as her SOUL or LIFE PURPOSE NUMBER. This tells us that while undoubtedly she will have the need to create, to manifest, to bring something into being, she will also be prevented from doing so at times by a crippling level of insecurity and self-worth. She will probably stop herself at the last moment from leaping the chasm from mediocrity towards greatness.

"Most THREEs will be able to recognize the many times they have walked away from something that could have been amazing just that one minute too soon… or have gone against their gut to trust their most brilliant ideas with the wrong people, only to see things come crashing to the floor."

She carries childhood experiences that may have created either expectations, beliefs or woundings about how the world operates, and how people behave, and she will be forced again and again to challenge these beliefs until she is able to come to a point of healing and understanding. The coping strategies and beliefs that she put in place as a little girl may well be appropriate in childhood, but they need to be assessed as to whether they are still valid for her in adulthood. Rosalie will need to challenge her inner child beliefs again and again, before she finds the point where she truly inhabits and determines her own beliefs.

Rosalie's purpose is to recognize the absolute power that sits inside of her, and not wait for others to recognize it or give permission for her to be powerful. Her purpose is to find her own sense of Self Worth. Once she is able to step into the power of her Self Worth, she will not only be able to create, to manifest, to develop anything she puts her mind to, she will be able to sustain it as well."

Our diagram has taken on a life of its own now!

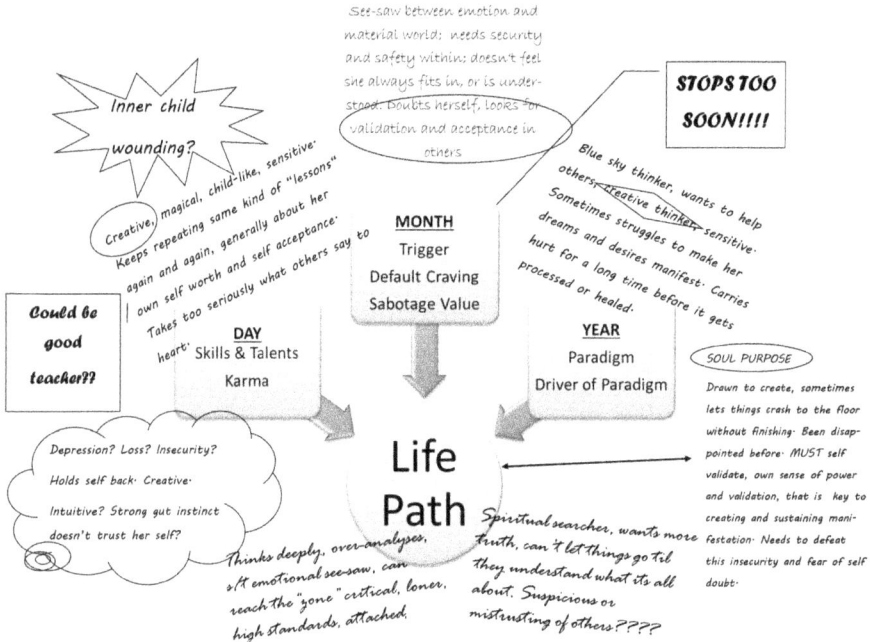

What Rosalie has to say

At this point Rosalie was quite amazed. She is very creative and has always made things – clothes, birthday cards, hand-made gifts. She has just recently started painting with oil and water paints, and finds that she is producing the most amazing artwork. "I go into another world when I draw or paint and lose all track of time," she says.

She also often finds herself starting things off from scratch… a woman's club for other immigrants when she found herself in a foreign country, a second hand clothing and shoe charity project for African-AIDS orphans, a support programme for women and children victims of Alcohol Abuse. "I am really very good at starting things but I either run out of steam, or things fall apart before they become really successful". Just recently someone told her that her art is good enough to be exhibited, but because of her past experiences where things fall apart at the last minute, she is scared of trying, and is holding herself back. "I really don't know whether my work is good enough, or I am strong enough to accept other people's criticism and comments," she says.

Rosalie is aware that she walks a fine line emotionally in trying to be part of the world, and trying to fit in. "In the past I have really struggled with both depression and anxiety, but am now learning meditation and attending self-discovery classes, which is helping me to learn about how to live an emotionally authentic life while still earning a living!"

"I do know there are times that I am so super-sensitive, and what people say about me affects me quite a lot. I brood about it for weeks, sometimes even months afterwards."

On loss: I have had some very profound losses in my life. The loss of my son, a marriage and my mother have all had a huge effect on my life. It is only now that I feel I am beginning to process and heal all of these endings through my painting.

On childhood wounding: Yes, this makes so much sense to me. I have spent so much energy in denying my childhood and running as far away from it as possible, without realizing that I was really running away from myself. It is only now in my late 30's that I feel strong enough to face and heal my childhood traumas.

Step Four: Working out the Universal and Personal Year Cycle

At the time of writing, this is 2013. If we add up the digits, i.e. 2 + 0 + 1 + 3 = 6, which gives us a Universal Year Energy of SIX.

$$2 + 0 + 1 + 3 = 6$$

The Universal Year is a SIX

As we have already learnt, a SIX is a year which signifies family, home and investment, so it also hones in our any investments we may have, any property issues regarding house or land, and long term financial planning that we need to do to take of our future safety.

The SIX energy often asks that we begin caring for ourselves FIRST before we can begin to care for those around us. By being aware of our needs and energy levels we then are more able to be able to support, encourage and care for others around us with compassion and non-judgment.

SIX years also place a large focus on the home, the land, and the family investment, and so it is a year where you need to pay attention to those long term investments and pension funds for your old age. This is the year to fix the house and make your home your space of refuge and calm in the world. This is also the year to fix the family relationship to what it is that YOU need, with honor and respect and compassion for all.

Rosalie comments: So funny, because I have spent this year clearing out and renovating my home, and making my home space into a place of peace and refuge. I had an urge to nest this year, and to look after myself, almost as though there were an inner voice whispering to heal, be gentle, take time out. Interestingly I have also had to sort out my pension funds and retirement funds this year! I have spent quite a bit of time connecting and visiting family and healing old ground. It feels as though it has been a year of forgiveness and healing, resting and recuperation more than anything.

It's unusual for me to spend so much time on my own. I normally need to be surrounded by people as I don't like feeling alone, but this year I have finally begun to feel comfortable "in my own skin". For the first time I think I am coming to terms with WHO I AM, and not who other people think I am, or expect me to be.

If we follow that same calculation, we can see that 2014 will be a 7 year, 2015 an 8 year and 2016 will be a 9 Universal Year.

This means that the focus will change over the next couple of years as the energy of the year changes. "Knowing how the energy of the years is going to change, and what areas and issues come into focus under the spotlight is really helpful for me," says Rosalie.

2014 asks that we reflect deeply on who we are, what we believe in, what our truth is, what collective truths about the society we live in that we have come to believe or disregard, what is it that holds real meaning or real value for us. It is a year where what is hidden or kept secret can become known, where secrets and lies become exposed for the untruth they really are, where the Media, Government and Community Leaders will be held accountable for what it is they ask us to believe. As we pull our attention inward and we examine our life, our purpose and our truths, it can inspire us to achieve our full potential in any situation. It is also a year of action and consequence, or seeing the results from our labours, of hard work and focus transforming to manifesting results.

2015 brings a global focus on money and the making, lending, borrowing, use of money. Power and the use and abuse of power comes into the spotlight, as it relates to political, corporate, governmental power… all the way down to the power that we spurn or appropriate in our own lives. In a good strong EIGHT cycle, this represents the culmination of all the work and discipline, creativity and knowledge of the previous seven years for the good of all on the planet; in a negative EIGHT year, it is all about power-mongering and money management which allows the rich to keep on getting richer and the poor to continue suffering. The EIGHT cycle challenges us to put our money literally where our mouth is, and take action.

2016 is a global year of completion. A NINE year asks us to wrap up and finish what needs to be completed with honor, so that we can start anew with new projects and focus areas in the new up-coming NINE year cycle. This means that on a global energy, communities and countries will be presented with the fruits of the labors over the past years, and asked to commit to finishing them. The alternative of *not finishing* means that we enter the beginning of the next NINE year cycle from an energy of non-completion and non-commitment, rather than one of fulfilment and success. Often a difficult year of challenge and assessment, we need to take care not to make excuses for non-performance and non-completion, or worse, blame it on someone else, all of which is highly possible in the energy this year brings.

Rosalie's Personal Year Cycle is a 9

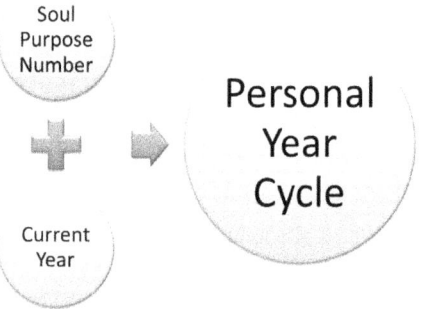

Rosalie's Soul Purpose value is a THREE, and the current year is 2013:

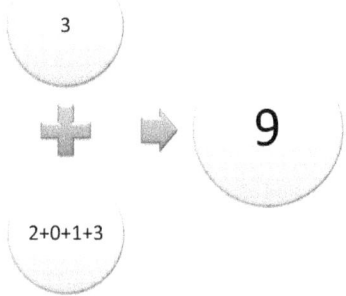

Her Personal Year is a NINE.

We know that NINE is a year of endings and completion, of assessing what works (and therefore keeping it) versus what no longer works (and needs to be released and let go). NINE signifies the energy of completion, in both Numerology and the Tarot. It is a natural ending, the small death so that rebirth can begin anew and the cycle can begin all over again.

The NINE year asks us to examine what we need to let go of, what needs to come to an end, in order that the new cycle of life can begin.

Rosalie knows better than most, that endings are not always neatly packaged like the last page of a novel, or a beautiful sun-set scene on the movie screen. Some endings are kind, gentle, and inevitable, but some are bloody, cruel, scarring us for years afterwards. "I finally am healing my own inner child woundings. For so long I have wanted the world to tell me that I am OK, that I DO matter, and now I realize that need has kept me trapped in insecurity and non-validation all my life. I almost have a subconscious expectation that I will be rejected because I don't fit in or am not good enough, and I am finally ready to explore that belief and heal it once and for all. I am ready to *be* someone new, to *do* things differently, to *let go* of beliefs and thought habits that no longer serve me. Before I would stop myself short of completing anything in case the project was a failure: in a weird way, if I hadn't finished it then it couldn't fail and so people couldn't disapprove of me… without realizing that the fundamental failure is in not allowing myself to try in the first place. Now I am completing my first series of paintings for an exhibition. Sure, I am as scared as all hell, but I am finally COMPLETING something for the first time in my life, not just STARTING something and letting it fizzle out half way through. It feels good. Scary, but good!"

Because I tend to be quite visual in the way I think, again I have created a diagram to help me see everything together in a conceptual visual.

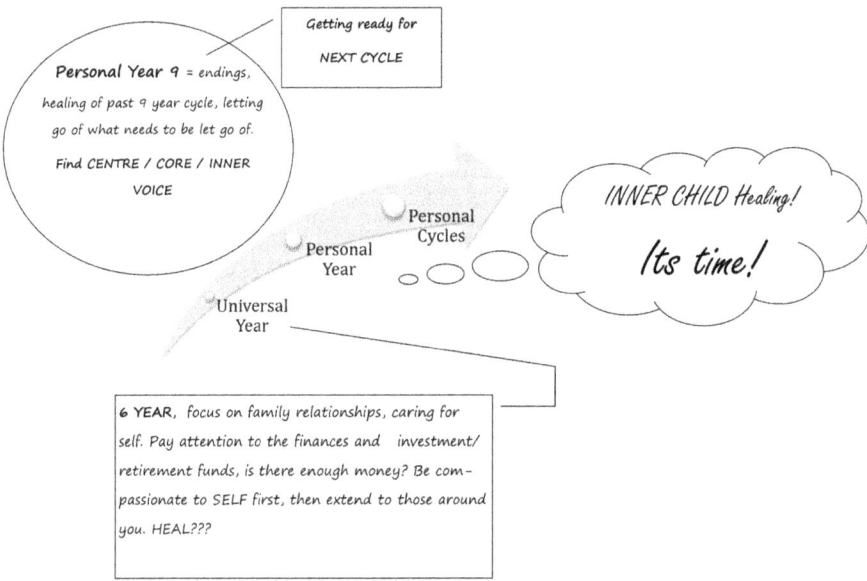

So there you have it: How to do a basic Numerhythm Analysis on someone. What do you need to do now? Practice, practice and practice some more - on ANYONE and EVERYONE who will let you. The more you play with the numbers, the more you will feel their rhythm and energy, and the more adept you will become!

In Conclusion

And so we have reached the end of this first part of our Numerhythms Adventure. By now, you are either completely hooked and want more information on the Numbers – or your eyes have glazed over, your head is hurting and you are feeling a little like you did way back when, sitting in the front row of Mr. Jones' maths class!

In this book we have learned the **Basics of Numerhythms** – how the values and patterns hidden in your date of birth reveal so much of who you are, if only you know how to look for the information.

But wait… There's more!!!

But of course, we have only explored the tip of the iceberg, and as always there is ALWAYS SO MUCH MORE to be discovered and learnt.

If you find yourself as intrigued and captivated by Numerhythms as I am, then you will want to travel further along this Grand Tour through the numbers with me.

Numerhythms, Your Life Code

This is what we have just worked through together in this book. By now you are familiar with terms and values such as Life Path, Soul Purpose, Talents and Skills, Paradigm Set, and Sabotage and Trigger Values. You have also been introduced to Universal and Personal Years, and have caught a glimpse into how we can use Numerhythms as a Descriptive AND a Predictive tool.

Numerhythms, Your Name Code

In this book we delve into the name that you carry, and what it reveals about who you are and how you grow. We look at your personality, your hidden dreams, your talents and skills, your sabotage values and so much more. We also look at married names, adoptive names and divorced names and learn what is revealed by each value. (To be released early 2014)

Numerhythms, Your Love Code

In this book we explore how to calculate compatibilities between personalities, and learn how to analyze the relationship challenges and strong points. (To be released early 2014)

Numerhythms, The Advanced Secrets of Intuitive Numerology

For me, this is where things begin to get really exciting. In The Life Code and The Name Code, we deal with very basic calculations in order to introduce the concept of working with the numbers. However, in Advanced Secrets of Numerology we ramp things up to a whole new level as we start to explore aspects like Compound Numbers, your Time and Location of Birth, and a fascinating section on Missing Numbers! We also start to look at past life karmic issues and how to examine a Numerhythms Time Line. (Date of release to be announced).

A SNEAK PREVIEW INTO ADVANCED SECRETS OF INTUITIVE NUMEROLOGY

About Compound Numbers

Does it make a difference if you were born the 8 April, or the 26 April? After all, both these numbers add up to a Skill and Talent value of 8. Would they have the same energy as someone born on the 17 April?

Or what about someone who is born in January, versus someone who was born in October? When we reduce the numbers we come to the same value of 1. Would their Triggers and Default Cravings be exactly the same, even though they were born 9 months apart?

In this book I have likened a Numerhythms reading to a painting, where each value and number adds a texture or shading to the picture. However, the finer detail on the picture which makes it come *truly* alive, the quality which defines it as a unique masterpiece comes from how the compound numbers interact and talk with each other *before* we reduce them to a single digit. For someone born on the 17 April, the 1 would tell us something, as would the 7, before we combine them to reach 8. Because of this they would be very different to someone who was born on the 26 April – the 2 would indicate a vital clue, as would the 6, even though the combined value in both instances is 8.

However this is quite advanced and, in order to fully grasp the power of compound numbers, we need to have a very good idea of exactly how the numbers behave together. For instance, why is 26 a good compound number in many ways? How do we deal with the range of emotional challenges and obstacles it brings with it?

Why does 17 sometimes bring inner conflict with it? They both add up to 8, but they give us two very different manifestations of the EIGHT energy.

Working With Time and Place

The **time** of your birth as well as the **place** of your birth both have powerful information to impart. Twins share the same date of birth, but they are most definitely not the same person. Why? Because even just a few minutes difference in birth time will impact on *HOW* you use your skills and talents, *HOW* you sabotage yourself, and *HOW* you relate to your Soul Purpose.

Our geographical place of birth impacts on the paradigm value (the year of birth) as well as how the Soul Purpose engages with the Personal Year. By now you are aware that Numerhythms is all about looking for the patterns within the numbers and how they are arranged. In **Numerhythms, The Advanced Secrets of Intuitive Numerology** we learn how to identify repetitive patterns and unravel the secrets they hold.

Past Life Secrets

By now you are aware that Numerhythms is all about looking for the patterns within the numbers and how they are arranged. In **Numerhythms, The Advanced Secrets of Intuitive Numerology** we learn how to identify repetitive past life patterns and how to resolve them.

Reading a Time Line

In this section I teach you how to create a Numerhythms Time Line, which illustrates how we are then able to read past events and predict future events, using Intuitive Numerology.

Missing Numbers

Missing Numbers? How does that work? In **The Advanced Secrets of Intuitive Numerology** we learn not only that it is what is seen that is relevant… but also the power of what is unseen, and how it impacts on the whole.

A New Journey

But for now, our journey in this book has come to an end. I hope that I have managed to convey to you just some of my passion and enthusiasm for this fascinating subject, and that you are now beginning to see the patterns and personalities of the numbers as they dance and twirl and parade in front of you in all aspects of your life.

Thank you for being part of my adventure! I hope to see you soon in the pages of another book in the Series of Numerhythms Books!

Acknowledgments and Thanks

Ask anyone who has ever written a book and they will probably tell you that the *easy* part of writing a book is the actual writing of it. The incredibly hard part is the editing and re-editing (many times over), the proof-reading and re-proof reading, (so many times that you can feel your eyes glazing over!), the typesetting and layout challenges, designing the cover, organizing the administrative aspect of it all – the list of things to do afterwards is mind-boggling and in my case, overwhelmingly daunting!

This book would not be here if it were not for some incredibly supportive people on my team:

To Franz for the typesetting and layout of the e-book and printed book. This book is very much a team effort. It might have my name on the cover, but it is only because of your technical knowledge, expertise and long hours of burning the midnight oil, that this book is now a reality.

To Rose, Joyce, Davy and Karl for proof-reading and re-proof reading. It's a hard job and needs as many pairs of eyes as possible to make sure that every t gets crossed and every i gets dotted. Thank you for dropping everything whenever I needed you to be my extra pair of eyes.

To my awesome kids who have learnt that the phrase "Mom is writing" is a euphemism for "make your own supper" and "bring another cup of tea please". Thank you for being so patient!

To my two Moms and supportive friends, Lana, Karen, Gisela, Sara, Beryl and Irene for helping me to develop the Cover Design for the book, and keeping me focussed on finishing what I started. Your feedback and support over this MAMMOTH project has been invaluable!

And last but by no means least: Thank you to the many hundreds and hundreds of clients who have allowed me to work with them in such intimate detail over the years. You are the inspiration for this work, and you are the ones who have helped me to hone this incredible gift that I have been given into my life's work. I thank you, each and every one of you, for being the most incredible teachers to me, and in turn, I dedicate this book to all of you. You know who you are! I am blessed, honoured and privileged beyond belief for the work you have allowed me to do with you.

ABOUT THE AUTHOR

Susan was born in England, but emigrated to South Africa with her family as a young child. She trained as a nurse after leaving school, but left to study journalism as she wanted to pursue a career in that field. She specialized in medical public relations, female health and general interest issues.

Throughout her life, Sue has been an avid lay-student of comparative religion, spirituality and self-development, and her interest in this field took her on an intensely personal journey of healing and psychic discovery. She studied metaphysics and spiritual psychology for many years with an Indian Guru and spiritual teacher in Johannesburg, drawn to energy healing for self and others, within the mental, physical, body, emotional and spiritual bodies.

Over the years she attended on-going diplomas and certifications, expanding her "counseling tool-box" namely: Ayurveda, Psychology, Nutrition, Journey Therapy, Spiritual Counseling, Energy Healing, Metaphysics, Emotional Freedom Technique, Imago Therapy, as well as the more esoteric aspects of psychic development and healing. She also became certified as a Neuro-Linguistic Programming Master Practitioner, obtaining her diploma through two years of intensive study.

Over the years, she has become recognized as a public speaker, and is frequently asked to present at conferences and spiritual gatherings; she has appeared on radio and TV many times, promoting her work. She has been an acclaimed metaphysical teacher since 2007.

She has been in private practice since 1999, providing services as an Intuitive Healer and Counsellor, firstly in Johannesburg, South Africa, and more recently in Munich, Germany. Her practice has evolved to become truly international over the past few years as even remote areas of the world have become technologically accessible. She advises clients of all ages and cultures from all over the world, from Australia and New Zealand to Alaska and Peru, and works with hundreds of people each year using Intuitive Numerology together with her other tools.

For more information about her work, please go to:

www.thesoullighthouse.com

www.ingramcontent.com/pod-product-compliance
Lightning Source LLC
Chambersburg PA
CBHW060823050426
42453CB00008B/564